Eyewitness to Majesty:

Abandoning Self for Christ

Peter

Eyewitness to Majesty:

Abandoning Self for Christ

Peter

Mindy Ferguson

AMG Publishers, Inc. | amgpublishers.com

Eyewitness Bible Studies

Eyewitness to Majesty: Peter, Abandoning Self for Christ

Copyright © 2012 by Mary Ferguson

Published by AMG Bible Studies, an imprint of AMG Publishers, Chattanooga, Tennessee (www.amgpublishers.com).

ISBN 13: 978-0-89957-909-2

First AMG Printing—December 2012

Cover art direction by Brian Woodlief, Chattanooga, TN.

Interior design by PerfecType, Nashville, TN.

Editing and proofreading by Rich Cairnes and Rick Steele

Printed in the United States of America

17 16 15 14 13 12 - VG - 7 6 5 4 3 2 1

DEDICATION

This study is dedicated with great gratitude to

the women of Cy-Fair Christian Church in Houston, Texas,

*whose encouragement and loving support spurred me
to believe God for this work.*

CONTENTS

Week 4: Humbling Encounters

Week 5: The Time Approaches

Week 6: Revealing Responses

Week 7: Defeat Gives Way to Victory

Week 8: Enlightening Revelations

Week 9: Refining Encounters

Week 10: Abandonding Self for Christ

Eyewitness To Majesty: Abandoning Self for Christ

The apostle Peter is mentioned more times in the four Gospels than anyone other than Jesus Christ Himself. Peter was praised more than any other disciple. He was also rebuked more than any other disciple. In our studies, we will see Peter fail and we will see him succeed. We will get a laugh or two at his expense, and we just may shed a tear or two with him. His imperfections make him lovable, and his victories give us hope.

Peter had a personal and intimate relationship with Jesus Christ. That relationship brought Peter to the point of abandoning not only his nets for Christ, but all his ambitions and selfish desires as well. The same relationship Peter had with Jesus is available to every believer who seeks to know Him as Savior and chooses to make Him Lord of her life as Peter did.

Through this study, we will walk along with Peter as an eyewitness to the life and majesty of Christ. We will watch Peter being transformed from Simon, the ordinary fisherman, to Peter, fisher of men. Peter will encourage you and inspire you. But most of all, he will challenge you to develop a deep and personal relationship with your Savior. He will motivate you to abandon self for Christ.

About This Study

During Peter's early ministry, he was accompanied by Mark. It is believed Mark wrote down Peter's teachings and translated them so they could be used to reach a more diverse audience. It is also believed Mark used the collection of Peter's teachings to write the gospel that bears his name. For this reason, the first seven weeks of our study will be based primarily upon the book of Mark.

In Week Eight, we will see the birth of the early church with its struggles and triumphs. In Week Nine and Week Ten, Peter will become our teacher as we learn the many lessons contained in his epistles.

Most of the lessons will take about thirty minutes to complete. Each unit is divided into five lessons designed to be done on a daily basis, five days a week. You will benefit most from doing the lessons one at a time, giving yourself time to reflect on each lesson before moving to the next one. Be sure to begin each session with prayer, asking God to speak specifically to you through the lesson. Make notes in the margin of anything you sense God is applying directly to a situation in your life. If you are doing the study with a group, these notes will make great discussion points when you get together to discuss your homework.

All quotations are from the New International Version[1] of the Bible, 1984 edition, unless otherwise noted. All Hebrew and Greek definitions are taken from the *Strong's Exhaustive Concordance of the Bible* unless another source is listed.

*We did not follow cleverly invented stories
when we told you about the power and coming of our Lord Jesus Christ,
but we were eyewitnesses of his majesty.*

2 PETER 1:16

Week 1
Revolutionary Meetings

Voice in the Desert

See, I will send my messenger,
who will prepare the way before me.

MALACHI 3:1

As we open the pages of our Bibles together and begin our study, let me explain why a Bible study focused upon the apostle Peter as an eyewitness to the life of Christ is based heavily upon the writings of the book of Mark.

> Mark wrote down Peter's teachings and was his interpreter.

Mark was an associate of the apostle Peter and, although he was not an eyewitness follower of Jesus, "He accompanied the apostle Peter and heard his preaching. Mark wrote down Peter's teachings and was his interpreter. He enabled Peter's teaching to reach a wider audience by translating his Aramaic discourses into Greek or Latin."[2] It is believed the major source of Mark's Gospel came from the apostle

Peter himself. So as we embark on this journey with the apostle Peter, we will spend much of our time together reading from the book of Mark.

Mark's gospel begins by highlighting the words of the prophet Isaiah.

Please read Mark 1:1–3.

Isaiah testified that a messenger would rise up in Israel to prepare the way for the Messiah. To begin our study, we will look at several passages of Scripture and allow God's Word to confirm the identity of John the Baptist as the one the prophets had been speaking of— the one who would prepare the way for our Lord and Savior, Jesus Christ ("Christ" is from the Greek for the Hebrew word "Messiah").

Please read Mark 1:4–8.

According to verse 4, where was John baptizing and preaching?

_____

Look back at Mark 1:3. How is the messenger described?

_____

John was the "voice of one calling in the desert." Let's take a look at the account of the birth of John the Baptist. These passages may be familiar to you, but read them this time for evidence of John's God-given purpose.

> John was the "voice of one calling in the desert."

Read Luke 1:5–17.

According to verse 17, the angel of the Lord indicated that John would go before the Lord in the "spirit and power" of whom?

_____

If you're like me, you're wondering exactly what was meant by "in the spirit and power of Elijah." Before moving forward, let's take a quick look at an incident involving the prophet Elijah that I believe reflects the spirit and power with which he served God.

Read 1 Kings 18:22–39.

What effect did the fire appearing on the altar have on the people?

_____

Has there been a time when someone's commitment and faith (maybe your own) was rewarded by God in a way that made Him more real to you? If so, please explain:

_____

_____

_____

_____

Our Lord is never too busy. He doesn't take a vacation. He doesn't sleep when we try to speak to Him. Elijah illustrated the futility of worshipping anyone other than the one, true God.

According to verse 37, for what purpose did Elijah ask God to answer him?

_____

_____

The people fell to their knees in reverence as they acknowledged the Lord of Israel as the true God. Elijah performed many miracles in his lifetime and was considered to be a great prophet, but his main purpose was to bring the people back to the Lord.

Another prophet named Malachi also made some predictions about the messenger who would precede the coming Messiah.

According to Malachi 3:1, what did the Lord say through the prophet?

_____

_____

Now compare Malachi 4:5–6 and Luke 1:17. What similarities do you find?

_____

_____

The name *Elijah* literally means "Jehovah is God."[3] His very name conveyed the fact that Elijah was commissioned to direct the people to the one, true God. Because of the prophecy in Malachi, the Jewish people were watching for Elijah's return as an indication that the Messiah (a king, anointed by God to redeem Israel) would soon come.

> The name *Elijah* literally means "Jehovah is God."

Read Matthew 11:11–15 and 17:10–13.

According to Jesus, who was John the Baptist?

Many of the people did not recognize that John the Baptist was "the Elijah" prophesied to come before the Lord did. John wasn't Elijah reincarnated, but he came "in the spirit and power of Elijah," just as the angel had told John's father, Zechariah, he would.

John lived in the desert, he prepared the way for the Lord, and, like Elijah, he served as a conscience for the people, calling on them to repent and return to God.

Interestingly, John even looked like Elijah. How is Elijah described in 2 Kings 1:8?

Now look back at Mark 1:6.

Those who were looking for the return of Elijah should have recognized that John the Baptist was the long-awaited messenger, a "voice calling in the desert" preparing the way for the Lord!

Tomorrow we will find that John the Baptist was also instrumental in Peter's life as we witness Peter's very first encounter with His soon-to-be Savior.

The Change

"Come, follow me," Jesus said, "and I will make you fishers of men."

MARK 1:17

*I*n yesterday's lesson we established through Scripture that John the Baptist was the messenger sent to prepare the way for the Lord. Today in our lesson, we will learn how John was also instrumental in Peter's life by examining the events that led to Peter's decision to leave his fishing nets behind in order to cast nets of infinitely greater significance.

Begin by reading Mark 1:9–13.

After being tempted, Jesus returned to the desert region where John the Baptist preached. It was then that Simon Peter had his first encounter with Jesus.

Please read John 1:35–42.

Who was Andrew, according to verse 40?_____

How was John the Baptist instrumental in Simon Peter's eventual call to be a disciple of the Lord?

_____

In verse 42, by what name did Jesus tell Simon he would be called?

_____

The name "Peter" in this verse is *Cephas* in Aramaic and it means "a stone or rock." Simon Peter spoke Aramaic and

> The name "Peter" in this verse is *Cephas* in Aramaic and it means "a stone or rock."

5

understood full well what the name meant. Jesus wasn't just giving him an insignificant nickname; He was changing Simon's very identity.

I can't help wondering what was going through Simon Peter's mind at that moment. In that culture, stones were used to construct buildings and homes. Boundaries were often marked with heaps of stones and stones had been used throughout Israel's history to memorialize God's activity in the lives of His people. I imagine Peter pondered Jesus' words well into the night.

Even though Peter couldn't have fully grasped the meaning of his new name at the time, he undoubtedly visualized a strong and significant object. At this point in Peter's life, he was anything but strong and significant. In fact, even the name "Simon" was extremely common.

What does Acts 4:13 tell us about Peter?

> Even though Peter couldn't have fully grasped the meaning of his new name at the time, he undoubtedly visualized a strong and significant object.

_____

Even though Simon Peter was ordinary and unschooled, Jesus saw the great spiritual leader this fisherman would one day become. I love that about our Lord. He meets us where we are, but sees our underlying potential. Throughout our study, keep in mind that every time Jesus referred to Simon as "Peter," He was reminding him (as well as others) of the kind of man Peter would one day become: a "rock," a significant and strong apostle for Jesus.

Read Mark 1:14–20 and write verse 18 here:

_____

Before reading further, let's look at Luke's account of the same event to gain a better understanding of how Peter came to the point where he was willing to respond so quickly to Jesus' invitation.

Read Luke 5:1–11.

Peter and his partners had been fishing all night and hadn't caught anything. My guess is that Peter didn't put his heavy, wet nets back in the water expecting to catch fish. I would imagine he was simply humoring Jesus. You can almost hear the reluctance in his voice: "Because you say so, I will let down the nets." But when the catch was more than Peter could have dreamed of even on a good day, he was overcome with emotion.

What did Peter say to Jesus in verse 8?

_____

_____

Encounters with Jesus Christ often reveal our desperate need to be redeemed. When Peter saw the abundance of fish Jesus had just enabled him to catch, he was overwhelmed by feelings of unworthiness. When Peter cried, "Go away from me, Lord; I am a sinful man!" he probably felt undeserving of the blessing and couldn't conceive that Jesus would accept him as he was.

The words "Go away from me, Lord" have probably been uttered by more of us than would like to admit it. As a teenager, I attended an event at which Billy Graham spoke. As he began preaching, I was instantly confronted with my sinful condition. I had sought to understand who God was for years. I wanted, more than anything else, to be loved and accepted. I went forward at the altar call, but I didn't truly give my heart to Christ. I began to question my decision even before I got to the bottom row of the stadium. I remained on the field until the invitation time was complete, but I left the event unchanged. In essence, I said, "Go away from me, Lord." I couldn't accept that God would love me. I heard the message and wanted what Dr. Graham described, but I pushed it away and continued living my life in the same manner. I didn't feel worthy of Jesus' love and was not ready to change.

What about you? Have you ever, through actions or words, told the Lord to go away? If so, briefly describe the circumstances:

_____

_____

_____

Although we are unworthy, if we listen rather than turn away, we will hear words similar to what Jesus told Peter in Luke 5:10. Write those words here:

_____

Peter was accepted. He didn't allow his feelings of unworthiness to stop him from responding to the Savior. Jesus understood that Peter was afraid. Peter had made an astonishing catch of fish, and now he heard that he and his partners would become "fishers of men."

When Peter was confronted with his sinful condition, he confessed it to Jesus; Jesus accepted him and promised to use Peter to bring others to do the same. Peter experienced the grace of God through Jesus, and his life was forever changed. He had a new name that reflected his future character, and he had a new profession that reflected his future passion.

> When Peter was confronted with his sinful condition, he confessed it to Jesus.

As we follow Peter's journey, we will witness the transformation that took place in his life. My prayer is that you will recognize changes in your own life and gain hope for God's continued work in you until the day you see Him face-to-face.

As a way of closing, read Philippians 1:6 and rejoice in the glorious promise it contains.

WEEK ONE — DAY THREE

The Great Physician

*"It is not the healthy who need a doctor, but the sick.
I have not come to call the righteous, but sinners."*

MARK 2:17

Yesterday we witnessed Jesus calling Simon, the fisherman, to become Peter, fisher of men. Today we will gain insight into some of the lessons Peter learned as he traveled throughout Galilee with Jesus. We won't talk specifically about Jesus' teachings, but instead focus more on the individuals He taught. If you're like me, I think you'll find some of them uncomfortably familiar.

Read Mark 1:21–34.

After leaving the synagogue, whose home did Jesus visit?_____

Who was sick at this home? _____

Jesus healed Peter's mother-in-law and she began to serve Jesus and his followers. The text doesn't indicate she rested for a while before waiting on her guests as we might expect. Instead, she immediately began to serve.

What do you think might have motivated Peter's mother-in-law to immediately serve the guests at her home?

_____

_____

_____

She might have felt a sense of obligation as most of us do when we have guests in our home, but I think there was more to it. Verse 31 tells us the woman "began to wait on them." The Greek word translated "wait" in this passage is *diakoneo* and it means "to be an attendant, i.e., wait upon." But it also means "minister (unto), serve." It is the same word used in Mark 10:45. Read that passage and note the context:

_____

Jesus came to serve. He served Peter's mother-in-law by healing her that day and she, in turn, served Jesus and His guests. Her service was evidence of her healing—she was physically able, but I would also guess this newly healed servant was gratefully willing.

Peter's mother-in-law probably served that day more from a sense of gratitude than obligation. When our acts of service are motivated by gratitude toward God, our perspective is right. Later that evening, she opened her home to the entire town, allowing others who needed healing to seek the same power of Jesus Christ she had experienced. That is a sincere spirit of gratitude and the mark of one who has truly been touched by Jesus. She couldn't keep Him to herself!

> Are you currently serving out of gratitude and love for your Lord?

Are you currently serving out of gratitude and love for your Lord? Do you sometimes serve out of a sense of obligation or in an effort to gain recognition? On the lines below, list all the ways you are currently involved in serving the body of Christ and note what motivates you to each act of service.

_____

_____

_____

I challenge you to serve out of gratitude to Jesus Christ. When you do, you'll find yourself giving far more graciously than you ever can when you serve from a sense of obligation.

Read Mark 1:35–39.

Everyone was looking for Him, yet Jesus was determined to "go somewhere else" to preach. Peter and the other disciples must have thought Jesus' response was very strange and wondered what He was thinking.

> I challenge you to serve out of gratitude to Jesus Christ. When you do, you'll find yourself giving far more graciously than you ever can when you serve from a sense of obligation.

News of the numerous healings had spread throughout the town of Capernaum. People were flocking after Jesus. Why would He leave just when He was gaining such popularity? Jesus came for all people, not just the ones in Capernaum. He had work to do and Jesus remained focused on His purpose.

Now read Mark 1:40–45.

The former leper certainly didn't heed Jesus' warning to keep his mouth shut. In fact, verse 45 tells us he went out and began to speak freely. As a result, Jesus could no longer enter a town openly.

Let's see what happened when Jesus returned to Capernaum.

Read Mark 2:1–12.

The crowd in the house was so large there was no room, even outside the door, to stand and hear Jesus speak. The people were so convinced of Jesus' power that a bold group of men were willing to dig through the roof in order to find for their friend a way into His presence.

Did you consider it strange that Jesus said, "Your sins are forgiven," rather than simply healing the paralytic? Sometimes we forget that physical healing is not the only healing a person might need.

When those men lowered the paralytic down through the hole in the roof, I imagine most everyone in the room assumed he was seeking physical healing. Because of Jesus' response to this man, it appears he suffered more from guilt and shame than from his physical challenges. To everyone's amazement, he received a physical healing and walked away with his mat. But I would guess it was the forgiveness he received that allowed this former paralytic to enjoy his restored condition. I'm sure there was a spring in that new step!

Peter and the other disciples had witnessed Jesus' healings and listened to His teachings as they traveled throughout Galilee. They learned their Leader had the power and authority to heal and to forgive. They also saw the now famous Teacher and Healer show compassion to the outcasts in their society, including a leper.

Now read Mark 2:13–17. What were Jesus' words in verse 17? _____

_____

_____

Peter and the other disciples needed to understand that the activities of the past few days were exactly what they could expect in following Him. The lepers, the demon-possessed, paralytics, and sinners would become familiar dining partners for this crew. But I imagine an uncomfortable silence came over the room as the disciples realized they, too, had been called because they were sinners. Jesus had not selected them because of their great credentials or righteous behavior, but because of their need for a spiritual doctor.

Read Romans 3:23 and note what you learn:

_____

_____

_____

Every one of us needs the healing only Jesus can give.

> Every one of us needs the healing only Jesus can give.

As a way of closing our lesson today, spend a few moments in prayer, thanking God He sent His Son to cover your sins and heal your soul. Jesus truly is our Great Physician!

11

A Higher Purpose

"For my thoughts are not your thoughts, neither are your ways my ways,"
declares the LORD.

ISAIAH 55:8

*T*oday we will cover some deep, thought-provoking material. Take a moment to pray before we start and ask for insight.

Read Mark 2:18–20.

In verse 19, how did Jesus describe His disciples?

_____

Jesus referred to Himself as the Bridegroom. Just as it would "be inappropriate for the groom's attendants to fast (an expression of sorrow) in the presence of the bridegroom, so it was inappropriate for Jesus' disciples to fast (in sorrow) while He was with them."[4]

At this time the disciples could not have understood that Jesus' bride would be the church—the very church these men would establish after Jesus was taken away from them. It is then that the disciples would be in need of fasting.

Now read Mark 2:21–22.

My sewing skills are almost nonexistent. As an adult, I've never tackled any more than attaching an occasional button, and the few sewing projects I attempted in my junior high school home economics class brought new meaning to the term "zigzag stitch."

But it doesn't take a seamstress to figure out you shouldn't use a piece of new, unshrunk cloth to patch a hole in an old garment. One wash and the patch would shrink and pull at the material. Likewise, new wine, which expands as it ferments, would burst old and brittle wineskins that were no longer flexible.

Read Romans 7:5–6 and note any insight you gain into Jesus' sewing analogy and His reference to new wine and old wineskins.

_____

_____

_____

The new way of the Spirit cannot be confined to the way of the law. The Pharisees were focused on the letter of the law. I would guess Jesus' words made the religious leaders quite uncomfortable. He continued to challenge their continual focus upon holding people to the letter of the law.

Read Mark 2:23–3:6.

When the Pharisees disapproved of the Lord feeding His people and healing on the Sabbath, they confirmed that Jesus' identity was a mystery to them. These religious leaders were so concerned with following the law they forgot why it was established in the first place.

> These religious leaders were so concerned with following the law they forgot why it was established in the first place.

Read some of the Sabbath laws recorded in Exodus 23:10–12.

What is the central theme of the Sabbath according to these verses?

_____

_____

The Sabbath was designed to allow God's people to rest and be refreshed. Interestingly, the "humanitarian aspect of the Sabbath law was ignored in Jesus' day."[5] These men were in the presence of the Lord Himself, but were so blinded by their focus on the letter of the law they couldn't see that healing and refreshment were among God's purposes.

In your experience, what happens when we focus too much on the law and forget to focus on the God who established the law?

_____

_____

We can certainly allow pride to raise its ugly head when we begin to hold others to the letter of the law. Pride appears to have taken hold of the hearts of the Pharisees.

According to Mark 3:6, how did the Pharisees respond to Jesus' correction?

_____

The zealous group evidently stirred up quite a ruckus in Jerusalem. Religious leaders started hunting Jesus down, and even His own family began to think Jesus had lost His mind.

Read Mark 3:7–30.

By whom did the teachers of the law say Jesus was possessed (v. 22)? _____

"Beelzebub" is another name for Satan.

What was Jesus' response in verse 23? _____

What the teachers of the law were proposing was absurd. Satan surely would not be casting out those who were in alliance with him. To do so would undermine his own work.

What did Jesus caution the religious leaders against in verse 29?

_____

_____

Although Jesus didn't directly say these leaders had committed this "eternal sin," it is clear that by observing the work of Jesus and attributing it to Satan, the men were in danger of "making a complete and final rejection of God's offer of salvation in Jesus."[6]

Just after Jesus' confrontation with the religious leaders, His family arrived.

Read Mark 3:31–34.

These are difficult words to swallow, especially for those of us who are mothers. To understand why Jesus would say such a thing, we have to keep in mind the purpose of His family's visit.

According to Mark 3:20–21, what did Jesus' family set out to do?

They were not there to see Jesus. They were there to stop Him! At that moment, they were opposing the will of God, and Jesus had no choice but to denounce their purposes. Without a doubt, Jesus loved His family. But they didn't understand what He was doing, and He couldn't allow them to undermine the work God had sent Him to do.

Read John 3:16–17.

Why did our heavenly Father send Jesus to Earth?

_____

_____

I am so thankful that Jesus never allowed anything to stand in His way! Jesus had a higher purpose than any of the people who opposed Him could not understand.

How does Isaiah 55:8–9 give you insight into the material we studied today?

_____

_____

_____

We covered a lot of material today. I encourage you to memorize Isaiah 55:8–9. The truth contained in these verses will give you courage and strength when you struggle to understand your circumstances.

Personal Application

*E*ach week you will spend your fifth day of study reflecting upon the material you covered in the previous four lessons. I encourage you to use this format to help you review and gain additional insight that will help you apply what you are learning to your everyday life.

Application from Day One

John the Baptist understood he was called to prepare the way for the Lord. He referred to himself as "a voice calling in the desert." Yet, he didn't fully understand his role until the end of his life.

If you're like me, you often try to figure out what God has planned before you act. We try to figure out where we will be a year from now, five years from now, etc. Yet God calls us to trust Him for today.

> If you're like me, you often try to figure out what God has planned before you act.

What does James 4:14 tell you?

_____

_____

We don't know how many tomorrows we have left in this life. We simply need to ask God to show us what to do for this day, and trust Him to handle all our tomorrows. I have a friend who often asks God to help her do "the next right thing." That is much easier said than done, of course.

I liken our spiritual walk to driving in the fog. When it is foggy, we can only see a few feet in front of our cars. We can make out blurred images of where we're going, but it is only by driving slowly and carefully, based upon what we can see at the time, that we get to our destination. As we drive, we continue to see the next few feet, as needed. If we try to see farther by turning on our bright lights, the light only reflects back at us, actually reducing our visibility.

God calls us to live our lives doing the next right thing for that day. He does sometimes gives us blurred visions of where we're going, but we usually don't clearly see the work He is accomplishing through us until we look back.

> God calls us to live our lives doing the next right thing for that day.

Are you stepping out in faith in some area of your life right now? If so, give a brief description:

_____

_____

Write a prayer of commitment to follow God and trust He will lead you through the "fog," step-by-step:

_____

_____

_____

Application from Day Two

When Jesus called Simon to be a disciple, He gave him a new name and a new purpose. Peter was a common, unschooled fisherman. He probably smelled of fish and had leathery, rough skin from years in the sun. Yet Jesus called him to lay down his nets and learn to minister to people from all backgrounds and economic levels. Peter probably felt more comfortable with the lepers than with the tax collectors. I would guess Peter wouldn't have been on the top of your recruitment list for a Sunday morning greeter. But Jesus called him to be a fisher of men.

The Lord does not expect us to have it all together to serve Him. As our relationship with Him grows, our lives begin to change. Even our outward appearance often changes.

Please read 2 Corinthians 5:17: "Therefore if any man *be* in Christ, *he is* a new creature: old things are passed away; behold, all things are become new" (KJV).

No matter where you come from or what you have done, you are never beyond the reaches of the grace of God. The Greek word for "new" in that verse is *kainos*. It denotes "new" as in "fresh." When you accept Jesus Christ as your Lord and Savior, you become a new creation. You get a fresh start!

> No matter where you come from or what you have done, you are never beyond the reaches of the grace of God.

Have you ever witnessed a transformation taking place in someone's life after that person came into a relationship with Jesus Christ? If so, describe what you saw:

_____

_____

What changes have taken place in your life as a result of your relationship with the Lord? Be specific. It's okay to boast as long as we are boasting in the Lord! Be prepared to share your answer with others if you are doing this study with a group.

_____

_____

_____

Application from Day Three

In our readings from Day Three, we focused on Jesus as the Great Physician. We saw Him heal the sick, forgive sins, and cast out demons. Most of us have probably experienced God in all three of these ways at one time or another. Let's celebrate His work in us by making note of a few of them.

1. Healing

Heal is defined as "to restore to health or soundness, to make well again."[7] A physical healing would return your body to health, and a spiritual healing would restore your spirit and soul to soundness.

Has there been a time in your life where you experienced physical or spiritual healing you attribute to the power of Jesus Christ? If so, explain:

_____

_____

_____

Jesus died to bring about your healing. Look at Peter's words regarding Jesus' suffering for your sake in 1 Peter 2:22–24 and note what you learn:

_____

Jesus paid the ultimate price to make you whole. If you've accepted Him as Lord and Savior, you've experienced His healing touch.

> Jesus paid the ultimate price to make you whole. If you've accepted Him as Lord and Savior, you've experienced His healing touch.

2. Forgiveness of Sins

The Hebrew word translated "forgive" is *calach* and it means "to forgive, pardon, spare." Pardon is defined as "to release from punishment; forgive an offense."[8]

If you have accepted Jesus Christ as your Savior, you have been pardoned. It's as though you never committed the offenses. Isn't that amazing?

Read Psalm 103:8–13. How far has God removed our transgressions (sins) from us?

_____

Write a brief description of your salvation experience or a time when your relationship with Christ became more personal.

_____

_____

_____

Take a moment to reflect on that experience and thank God for the people who were involved in your spiritual growth. If you've never formally thanked them and you know how to contact them, call or write a note to let them know how God used them to impact you.

3. Casting Out Demons

Okay, before you determine I have lost my mind and put this Bible study on the shelf, let me explain. For this application we are going to refer to the things we have been most afraid of in our lives as our "demons."

Every one of us has fears that have hindered our spiritual life in one form or another. One fear I have dealt with my entire life is the fear of speaking or singing in public.

> Every one of us has fears that have hindered our spiritual life in one form or another.

As a young adult, I took voice lessons for about a year. I did all the exercises and learned the proper techniques. But every time I stood before a microphone, my voice trembled, my knees knocked, and sometimes my teeth would even chatter. It was horrible. After numerous attempts to overcome the intense fear, my voice coach looked me in the eye and told me I needed to figure out what the source of my fear was or I would not make any progress. My husband and I were newly married, and the forty dollars a week I was spending on lessons was a sacrifice. Feeling defeated, I decided to stop the lessons.

I became a Christian a few years later and began to sense God's leading to sing again. I struggled terribly, but slowly overcame my fear by focusing not on myself, but on my Savior and His message. I eventually sang regularly on my church praise team. Today, I am rarely involved in leading worship, but speak frequently at women's events and Bible studies. Amazingly, I can now stand at a microphone without the familiar sounds of my knees knocking and teeth chattering. I still get a queasy stomach before speaking to new groups, but I have made incredible progress thanks to the all-sufficient grace of our Lord Jesus Christ.

What about you? What "demons" have been cast out of your life by the power of Jesus Christ?

_____

_____

_____

Application from Day Four

Jesus was continually being confronted because He did not go along with the ways of the world around Him. His own family was convinced He was out of His mind, and resolved to "take charge" of Him.

Read the following Scriptures and write down what they say about the ways of the world:

Colossians 2:8 _____

1 John 2:15–17 _____

Romans 12:2 _____

On the lines below, identify some areas in your life where you are being called to go against the ways of the world. If you can't identify any, ask God to show you what changes you need to make. Use these lines to write a prayer.

_____

_____

_____

The Lord called Peter to do many things the world did not understand. What key lessons did Peter learn from Jesus from which you believe he could draw?

_____

_____

Next week we will learn how Jesus prepared Peter and the other apostles for a ministry journey on their own.

Week 2

Valuable Instruction

WEEK TWO | **DAY ONE**

Seedtime and Harvest

As long as the earth endures, seedtime and harvest, cold and heat, summer and winter, day and night will never cease.

GENESIS 8:22

We will begin our second week of study by focusing on a few of the parables Jesus told in His popular teaching spot by the Sea of Galilee. These stories may be familiar to you, but I encourage you to imagine yourself sitting along the shore of the lake, hearing the stories straight from the mouth of the Master for the first time.

Read Mark 4:1–20 and fill in the chart below. I've done the first one for you.

> I encourage you to imagine yourself sitting along the shore of the lake, hearing the stories straight from the mouth of the Master for the first time.

Soil Descriptions from Mark 4:3–8	Explanation from Mark 4:14–20
1. Path	1. As soon as they hear the Word, Satan comes and takes it away from them.
2.	2.
3.	3.
4.	4.

The Word of God is like seed planted in the soil of our hearts. The seed has the potential to produce a fruitful crop; however, the condition of the heart in which it is planted determines its level of productivity or yield.

Let's look at what Scripture has to say about sowing seeds and reaping a harvest.

Read Genesis 1:11–12.

According to these verses, when you plant a seed in the ground, what kind of fruit can you expect to harvest?

_____

_____

Seed produces fruit that contains additional seeds, which bear fruit of the same kind. Likewise, God's Word (spoken or written) sown in our hearts always has the potential to produce a harvest (another heart more conformed to the image of the Word made flesh). It is the principle of seedtime and harvest.

Now read Genesis 8:22.

How long will the principle of seedtime and harvest continue?

_____

Jesus was preparing the disciples, specifically the twelve apostles, to go out and spread the seed of His Word. Jesus wanted to prepare the inexperienced crew to encounter on their journey each of the four types of people described in His parable. The apostles could control how much seed they planted, but they could not control the harvest.

Whether you have an evangelistic green thumb or are just beginning to share God's Word, there is much to learn from Jesus' parable of the sower. We'll make the principle of seedtime and harvest the primary focus for the next two lessons.

> Whether you have an evangelistic green thumb or are just beginning to share God's Word, there is much to learn from Jesus' parable of the sower.

Those with hearts like a path (hard and difficult to penetrate) have the Word scooped up by Satan so it never has the opportunity to take root and bear fruit. Those with hearts like rocky places accept the Word with great enthusiasm on the surface, but do not allow it to take root and grow. They fall away quickly when circumstances get tough.

According to Mark 4:17, what can people encounter because they have God's Word planted in their hearts?

_____

_____

Some trouble and persecution actually comes because of the Word. It is dangerous to teach that believers will never encounter trouble or hard times. That is simply not true. As a matter of fact, during seasons of tremendous spiritual growth, it is predictable that one will also encounter many difficulties and trials.

What does James 1:2–4 reveal to us about trials?

_____

_____

Take a moment to reflect on some of the trials you have endured in recent years. Write down some ways you have matured as a result of those experiences:

_____

_____

_____

Jesus said that, in addition to paths or rocky places, sometimes the seed we sow falls among thorns—those with hearts that desire the things of the world more than the things of the Spirit. A thorny heart hinders a person's ability to truly focus on the Word. The result is much like that of planting a seed among thorns. It is choked out, unable to grow.

Thankfully, in the course of our planting we will discover that some seed falls on fertile soil, which represents those with hearts ready for the message and aware of their need to change. People with fertile hearts allow the Word to penetrate deep, take root, and grow.

According to John 1:1, 14, who is the Word? _____

_____

The Word, Jesus Christ, is the Seed planted in us who takes root and bears fruit according to His kind, transforming us into His image. We, in turn, spread seed by sharing the Word with others, and the process continues. Seedtime and harvest. This is the mark of a mature Christian, the goal for every one of the apostles, and the goal for all of us as believers in Christ.

> The Word, Jesus Christ, is the Seed planted in us who takes root and bears fruit according to His kind, transforming us into His image. We, in turn, spread seed by sharing the Word with others, and the process continues.

There is a difference between a disciple and an apostle. *Disciple* "implies the acceptance in mind and life of the views and practices of the teacher."[9] But *apostle* denotes a "messenger, or delegate, dispatched with orders."[10] Many disciples followed Jesus during His ministry, but He appointed only twelve as apostles.

Re-read Mark 3:13–19.

The apostles were disciples who had learned and accepted Jesus' teachings and were commissioned by Him to be messengers of the Good News of salvation available through Him. They were dispatched to sow seeds that would in turn bear more fruit according to its kind. The journey Peter and the other apostles took with Jesus began with discipleship, but prepared them for their ultimate role as apostles.

That concludes our lesson for today. Tomorrow we will focus on other parables taught at the lake and determine their significance in preparing Peter and the other apostles to sow the seed of God's Word throughout the land.

WEEK TWO · DAY TWO

Preparing to Sow

Night and day, whether he sleeps or gets up, the seed sprouts and grows, though he does not know how.

MARK 4:27

Yesterday we discussed the parable of the sower and its significance for the twelve apostles. Today we will look at other parables taught by Jesus at the water's edge. Kick your shoes off and get comfortable. The Master has much to teach us today!

Read Mark 4:21–25.

Jesus is the Lamp who reveals what is hidden in the hearts of men. It is the condition of the heart that enables one to have eyes that see and ears that hear. Our job is to sow seeds, nurture them, and love people until their hearts are ready to accept the Word and let it grow. We are not called to judge.

What words of caution are expressed in Mark 4:24?

> Jesus is the Lamp who reveals what is hidden in the hearts of men. It is the condition of the heart that enables one to have eyes that see and ears that hear.

_____

_____

Now read Matthew 7:1–2 and Luke 6:37–38.

The parable of the sower showed us that the condition of the heart determines the crop. Jesus cautioned His listeners to be careful. They were called to be faithful and give without judgment. They also needed to be prepared for others to judge them harshly.

Read 1 Corinthians 4:1–5 and note any additional insight you gain about the dangers of judging the hearts of others:

_____

_____

We are called to simply continue planting the Word. When the Lord returns He will judge and expose the motives of men's hearts, both those who sow seed and those who hear the message. Only the light of Christ can expose the true motives of men.

Re-read Mark 4:25.

Ultimately, those who accept and have the Word growing in their hearts will experience more of the Word (Jesus) in heaven. However, for those who do not have the Word growing in their hearts, even what seed they have received will be taken away and they will be separated from the Word for all eternity.

Why do you think Jesus intertwined the subject of sowing the seed of His Word with teaching about the dangers of judgment?

_____

_____

> Isn't it our nature to judge based on results?

Isn't it our nature to judge based on results? Jesus had made it clear He came for sinners. He was preparing the twelve apostles for their mission and knew their tendency would be to judge the hearts of those to whom they preached. He also knew they would be inclined to judge their own success based on results. But God's methods are different from those of the world.

Now read Mark 4:26–34.

The kingdom of God would grow, but in such a way that the twelve apostles would not understand. It would begin with a small group of men committed to the cause, but the Kingdom would eventually grow large and strong. They were not to measure results based on human understanding.

The Word will continue to produce fruit until the final harvest of believers. There is an appointed time for that harvest.

When evening came and the teaching was over for the day, Jesus had His disciples weigh anchor push the boat out to sea and head to the opposite side of the lake.

Read Mark 4:35–41 and try to picture in your mind the scene.

Boats at that time usually had a large triangular sail, which was attached to a wooden support and suspended on a central mast so it could be moved to catch the wind. Steering was from the rear, with a large oar that acted as a rudder.[11]

How is the storm described in verse 37? _____

The intense storm came up quickly. The disciples probably scrambled to maneuver the boat as chaos broke out.

Where was Jesus sleeping (v. 38)? _____

The book of Mark tells that Jesus was asleep in the rear portion of the boat on a cushion. More than likely the disciples scurried around the boat trying to steady it. But we can assume it would be rather difficult to steady a boat without the help of the man at the rudder! The disciples were exasperated that Jesus was not helping. Didn't He care if they drowned? As the waves crashed over the sides and the disciples woke Jesus, they were probably expecting Him to grab the rudder and help stabilize the boat. When He stood and calmed the storm itself, I expect it was not only the waves that stood still, but His entire astonished crew as well.

When was the last time you felt as if the Lord was sleeping on a comfy cushion while your life was in chaos?

_____

_____

_____

Jesus cares when your life is in chaos. In our humanness, we panic and leap into action, many times without even a prayer. But Jesus knew the disciples would make it to the other side, so He was at total peace amid the chaos.

Where did Jesus say they were to go in verse 35? _____

The disciples needed to learn that when Jesus told them something, they could count on it. Whatever "storms" might come against them, if Jesus said they would get to the "other side," that is exactly where they would end up.

> The next time a "storm" rages in your life and you feel as if the Lord is not taking action, find comfort in knowing He has absolute authority over all Creation.

The next time a "storm" rages in your life and you feel as if the Lord is not taking action, find comfort in knowing He has absolute authority over all Creation. You may not be able to join Him on a comfy cushion while the waves of life crash around you, but as a believer you can have faith He will take you to the other side.

Read Mark 5:1–20.

In addition to the elements of nature, what does Jesus have authority over?

_____

What authority does Jesus demonstrate in the events recorded in Mark 5:21–43?

_____

Jesus demonstrated His absolute authority over the elements of nature, evil spirits, animals, sickness, and even death. Authority is defined as "the right to command, enforce obedience, and make decisions."[12]

In a traffic jam, when a police officer directing traffic sticks out his hand and says, "Stop!" why does the car coming toward him obey?

_____

_____

The driver of the car knows that if he doesn't stop, he will more than likely receive a ticket with a hefty fine, not to mention have charges filed against him if he injures the officer. The officer, because of the authority he possesses, has the power to enforce the law and tell the driver what to do. What might happen if the policeman were not in uniform and the driver were not able to recognize him as an officer of the law?

Would the officer have any less authority? No, but his authority wouldn't be as effective. Jesus encountered a similar experience.

Read Mark 6:1–6.

Why was Jesus unable to perform many miracles in His hometown?

Jesus' family and friends did not recognize His authority; therefore, His authority was far less effective.

When we show a lack of faith in the Lord's ability to accomplish His purposes in our lives, aren't we doing the same thing? Is He able? You'd better believe it. But unless we acknowledge His authority over all Creation, including the matters that concern us on a daily basis, we will not experience the full benefit of His power. How do we grant Jesus authority? Through obedience. Our level of obedience to the Word and our ability to recognize His sovereign authority determine the effectiveness of His authority in our lives.

We have seen how Jesus prepared the apostles to plant the seed of His Word, to avoid judging based on results, to trust Him to bring about the harvest, and to have faith in His authority over all Creation. Our Lord has authority over all things, but we have free will to operate under that authority or outside it.

Based upon what you've learned today, are there any changes you need to make in order to better grant Jesus authority over your life? Note your thoughts:

We have read some thought-provoking teaching today. In tomorrow's lesson, we will see how the apostles fared as they worked the field of souls for the very first time.

Tending the Flock

There they will lie down in good grazing land, and there they will feed in a rich pasture on the mountains of Israel.

EZEKIEL 34:14

*I*n our lesson yesterday, Jesus taught by the lake, calmed a storm, and demonstrated His authority over all Creation. Jesus continued to teach in the villages throughout the region and as we open our Bibles for today's lesson, we'll find Him commissioning the apostles for their first mission.

Begin today by reading Mark 6:6–13.

Jesus sent the apostles out, two by two, to preach to the people. He passed on His authority to them as His representatives. They had been prepared by Jesus' teachings and were beginning to apply some of what they had learned.

The text doesn't tell us specifically why Jesus sent the disciples out in pairs, but perhaps it was because they were called to be witnesses to the power and authority of Jesus.

What does Deuteronomy 19:15 indicate is required for a matter to be established?

The apostles had witnessed all the miracles Jesus had performed. They had seen Him heal the sick, cast out demons, and raise the dead. But to convince others, there needed to be two witnesses.

What other reason might Jesus have had for sending the Twelve out in pairs (Matthew 18:20)?

In yesterday's lesson we learned that Jesus had authority over nature, evil, sickness, and even death. He passed on His authority to the apostles, and He was with them in Spirit during their travels. Some people certainly didn't welcome the apostles; others probably wouldn't listen. But as you will see from our next reading, these men definitely made an impact.

Read Mark 6:14–29.

The apostles' activities were the talk of the town, and Herod heard about it. He was terrified by the prospect of John the Baptist rising from the dead. I don't know if the execution of John the Baptist affected you as it did me, but I am so struck by the acts human beings are capable of just to protect their pride.

> I don't know if the execution of John the Baptist affected you as it did me, but I am so struck by the acts human beings are capable of just to protect their pride.

What does verse 20 say Herod liked to do? _____

Herod had probably listened to John often and he recognized that John was a righteous and holy man. Prior to the banquet, Herod had protected John. Yet, when confronted by his stepdaughter (and niece) at a gathering of his subordinates, Herod ordered John to be beheaded without dignity, purpose, or reason.

Have you ever allowed your pride to cause you to do something you wouldn't do under normal circumstances? If so, describe the circumstances:

_____

_____

_____

_____

Read Psalm 73:6–7 and Proverbs 11:2.

Take a moment and ask God to prompt you in the future through His Holy Spirit whenever you are motivated by pride. Ask Him for the courage to swallow that pride, and seek His counsel before proceeding.

The apostles got the attention of many, and they did well on their first mission trip. Jesus attempted to reward them with rest from the crowds.

Let's see what happened. Read Mark 6:30–44.

Would you feel compassionate toward these people or would you be annoyed they had interrupted your quiet time of rest with the Lord?

_____

I think it's safe to assume most of us would be at least slightly irritated at the interruption. But Jesus had compassion on the people because they were like sheep without a shepherd, lost and in need of a leader. They had come seeking Him, and He gave without hesitation.

How does Jesus refer to Himself in John 10:14? _____

Jesus gave the people compassion, instruction, and nourishment. He is the Good Shepherd and tended to the flock's every need that day—with a basketful of evidence for each of the apostles.

Mark leaves out some important details relating to Peter. So, our final reading today is from Matthew.

Read Matthew 14:22–36.

Peter's failures encourage me and challenge me. There have been many times I have raced forward in total faith, full of anticipation of all God was going to accomplish in and through me. Yet fear has often hindered my ability to walk with my Savior when the winds of life roar past.

According to verse 31, what did Jesus do when Peter allowed fear to wash out his faith?

_____

> Take a moment and ask God to prompt you in the future through His Holy Spirit whenever you are motivated by pride.

Oh, how I praise our Lord that He reaches out immediately to catch us! Jesus knew Peter would fall before he ever stepped out of that boat. But He also knew that that brief faith walk would be an experience Peter would draw from for many years to come.

> Oh, how I praise our Lord that He reaches out immediately to catch us!

Jesus is always there to catch us when we fall. Don't be so afraid of failing that you forego the moments of "walking on the water" with your Lord!

The Blessed Walk

He that hath clean hands, and a pure heart; who hath not lifted up his soul unto vanity, nor sworn deceitfully. He shall receive the blessing from the LORD, and righteousness from the God of his salvation.

PSALM 24:4–5 KJV

After Jesus fed thousands by the lake, the disciples picked up the leftovers, probably amazed at the abundance that remained. Then Jesus urged the disciples to get back into the boat.

Read Mark 6:45–56.

According to verses 51 and 52, what was the reason the disciples had been "completely amazed"?

_____

_____

Please read John 6:16–35 in order to gain a little more insight into the significance of the loaves.

Who is the Bread of Life? _____

Jesus taught that though the Israelites ate manna (bread) from heaven, they still died. The bread sustained them and met their temporary physical needs. However, Jesus would give His flesh, which would be broken (like the five loaves) so it could meet the needs of the multitudes. This time, rather than sustaining His people for a temporary season, God would supply their needs for all eternity in heaven. The disciples should have recognized that Jesus was the Messiah by His miraculous feeding of the five thousand.

Jesus possessed the same authority and power over all Creation as His Father. He demonstrated that authority when He walked on water. God has always had authority over water; He created it. He brought the great flood waters in Noah's day, parted the Red Sea as the Israelites fled Egypt, and parted the waters of the Jordan River, allowing His people to pass through to the Promised Land.

Had the disciples fully understood that Jesus is the Bread of Life and the Son of God sent straight from heaven, they would have understood He was the long-awaited Messiah. They would not have been amazed as He walked on the water as though it were a shimmering sapphire pavement.

> Jesus possessed the same authority and power over all Creation as His Father. He demonstrated that authority when He walked on water.

I can't help but wonder if Jesus was reminiscing of times with His Father in heaven as He walked on surface of the lake. What did Moses and the other leaders of Israel say was under the feet of God in Exodus 24:9–10?

_____

_____

Oh, how I wish I could experience just a moment on that water with Jesus! In yesterday's lesson we saw that Peter did just that. One of the characteristics of Peter that I enjoy most is his enthusiasm and earnest desire to experience all he could of his Lord. What about you? Would you be the one hollering out to Jesus, "Tell me to come to you on the water"?

When was the last time you jumped out of the safety of a "boat" to take a risk and walk with the Lord in a whole new way?

_____

_____

_____

If your answer was "never," that's okay. But take a moment to ask God to reveal His activity around you. And when He reveals it, get out of the boat and join him! Get out of your comfort zone. You just may find it wasn't as comfortable as you once thought. The blessings will be endless!

Read Mark 7:1–23.

According to verse 8, what did Jesus say the Pharisees and teachers of the law were letting go of in order to hold on to the traditions of men?

_____

Can you think of any of God's commands our society has traded for modern-day traditions or customs?

_____

_____

_____

_____

Jesus was disturbed because the Pharisees were so focused on appearing clean on the outside that they gave no thought to the condition of their hearts. They spoke of the law and they taught the law, all in the name of serving God. But their hearts cherished the legalism of their traditions more than the God they professed to serve.

Re-read Psalm 24:4–5 from the King James Version at the beginning of this lesson.

Who receives blessings from the Lord?

_____

The Pharisees were focused on clean hands, but didn't give attention to the condition of their hearts. God is far more interested in the purity of our hearts than our outward appearance.

Re-read Mark 7:17–18, then read Matthew 15:10–20.

Who asked Jesus to explain the parable?_____

Mark does not tell us it was Peter to whom Jesus referred when He said, "Are you still so dull?" I guess Peter must have decided to leave out that tidbit of information as he preached! I really enjoy Peter. His enthusiasm usually caused him to speak up before anyone else. He was also apt to get corrected more than the other apostles, as we will see later in our study. Peter probably would have liked to forget some of those times when he boldly stepped forward before thinking, but I sure take comfort in them. If Peter could become the leader of the apostles and overcome his uncanny ability to say the wrong thing at the wrong time, we all have hope!

Peter walked on water with Jesus, but he also walked with Him every day, learning and growing. Peter had a heart for Jesus and I believe the walk itself was his greatest blessing!

> Peter walked on water with Jesus, but he also walked with Him every day, learning and growing.

WEEK TWO — DAY FIVE

Personal Application

Application from Day One

On Day One we examined the four basic reactions to the Word of God as described in the parable of the sower. Look back at the chart on page 24 and following pages and fill in the blanks:

1. Heart like a _____.

Hear the Word, but Satan comes immediately to take the Word that was sown.

2. Heart like a _____ place.

Receive the Word with joy, but fall away quickly during trouble or persecution.

3. Heart crowded with _____.

Hear the Word, but worries, wealth, or worldly desires choke it out.

4. Heart like _____ soil.

Hear the Word and accept it, producing an abundant crop.

Take a moment to reflect on your own life. Of the four reactions listed, how many have you experienced at one point or another? _____ Explain:

_____

_____

_____

_____

Which soil type most closely describes your heart condition at this time?

_____

You may be in the heat of a trial, wondering if you will endure and remain with this "Christianity" thing. It may be that you are more focused on the things of the world than of the Spirit and are feeling defeated and confused. Perhaps you can rejoice because you have a deep desire to be transformed into the likeness of Christ and can see evidence of spiritual fruit. Regardless of your current condition, take a moment and ask God if there are changes you need to make in order to reap the abundant harvest of the "fertile soil." Make any notes in the margin.

> Regardless of your current condition, take a moment and ask God if there are changes you need to make in order to reap the abundant harvest of the "fertile soil."

According to Romans 12:2, how are we transformed?

_____

_____

All changes start with a conscious decision—a change of action, a change in thought. Then the heart changes.

Read Romans 8:29–32.

You were predestined to be conformed to the likeness of Christ. Allow the seed planted within you to bear fruit according to His kind by transforming you into His image. It is your destiny!

Application for Day Two

In the latter part of Day Two's lesson, we discussed the importance of recognizing God's authority.

Re-read Mark 6:1–6.

Jesus didn't perform many miracles in His hometown because His family and neighbors did not recognize His authority. His authority didn't change, but because the people would not listen and obey Him, His authority was far less effective. Unless we allow Jesus Christ to be Lord over every area of our lives, we will not experience the true potential of His authority and power. So let's delve into what it means to give Jesus Lordship over our lives.

The Greek word most often used for "lordship" is *kurieuo*. It means "to rule: have dominion over, lord, be lord of, exercise lordship over" and it is translated "lordship" or "dominion." Our Lord needs to rule our marriages, our other relationships, our work, our service, even our thoughts.

What does 2 Corinthians 10:5 indicate we are to do with our thoughts?

_____

_____

_____

Yes, we even need to grant Christ lordship over our thoughts. If our views and feelings do not agree with the Word of God, they are not in obedience to Christ and will diminish His power in our lives.

On page 31, I asked you to note any changes you need to make in order to better grant Jesus Lordship over your life. Look back at your answer.

Now I encourage you to write a prayer of commitment, granting Jesus Lordship over every area of your life, particularly with regard to the changes you listed. Your new commitment may require letting go of some things you are used to controlling, but anything we cling to more tightly than we cling to Jesus Christ only hinders our growth and undermines His work in us. Write your prayer:

_____

_____

_____

_____

_____

Application for Day Three

In Day Three we witnessed Jesus tending to His flock. He knew the needs of each individual present at the lake. He didn't just see a crowd. Jesus knew every man, woman, and child who partook of the loaves that day. He knew their thoughts, their hurts, and their desires. Jesus is the Good Shepherd and He knows His flock.

Read John 10:2–4.

You are one of Jesus' sheep and He knows you by name. Write Jesus' words recorded in Matthew 10:30:

_____

_____

_____

The Lord knows you that well!

One of my favorite passages of Scripture is Psalm 23. Take a moment to read it and record below the attribute of your Shepherd that means the most to you at this time.

_____

If you are in a deep financial crisis and don't know how you will make it, you "shall not be in want." If you are tormented by shame and guilt or feel far from your Savior, "He restores." If you are sick, in pain, or have recently lost a loved one, though you "walk through the valley," He is with you. And if this life simply seems too much for you to bear, take heart in knowing that as a believer you "will dwell in the house of the LORD forever." He knows your every hurt and sees every tear. He knows how to meet your needs, big and small. He is your Good Shepherd and He knows you that well.

> If this life simply seems too much for you to bear, take heart in knowing that as a believer you "will dwell in the house of the LORD forever."

Application for Day Four

In Day Four's lesson, the Pharisees received a strong rebuke from the Lord. They talked a good talk, knew all the "religious" jargon, but their hearts were far from God. Their focus was on their outward appearance, and they had become so absorbed with observing traditions that those traditions became void of any spiritual value.

Does your family observe any traditions you are passionate about? If so, describe them:

> Does your family observe any traditions you are passionate about?

_____

_____

The tradition that came to my mind is gift-giving at Christmas. Gift-giving was originally established during the Christmas season as a symbolic reminder of the gift God gave us in His Son, Jesus. But for many, the gifts themselves have turned into the focal point of the entire holiday. For much of society, even Christmas carols have become void of their true meaning.

Take a moment to evaluate your family traditions, both at Christmastime and throughout the year. Are there any adjustments you need to make? If so, write them down:

_____

_____

_____

Ask God to help you remember to keep your heart focused on Him, including making Him the focus of every celebration.

That concludes our second week of study. I am praying that God will speak to you specifically through your time in His Word. Is there something that convicted you this week, or something you were able to apply immediately? If so, write about it and if you are doing this study with a group, be ready to share your answer:

_____

_____

_____

_____

Week 3

Compassion at Work

Healing Compassion

The LORD is gracious and compassionate, slow to anger and rich in love.
The LORD is good to all; he has compassion on all he has made.

PSALM 145:8–9

*J*esus is compassionate and He loves deeply. As we begin our third week of study together, we will witness His compassion as He encounters two very different people in two completely different situations. When Jesus went to the vicinity of Tyre and Sidon, He was trying to keep His presence a secret. The crowds had followed Him wherever He went and Jesus continually reached out to them. But this day, our Lord wanted some time alone with His disciples, apparently to instruct them.

Please read Mark 7:24–30.

Jesus is the Bread of Life and the Word made flesh. But His disciples were His first priority at the time. He was feeding them spiritually (teaching) and didn't want to take from their plates to minister to the woman until they were satisfied.

In verse 27, how did Jesus refer to the woman? _____

To you and me, this sounds like an insult. But, given Jesus' compassionate nature, that response would be inconsistent with His character. So what did He mean? The woman's comments give us some insight.

When a family sits down to a meal, the parents do not take food from the children's plates and give it to the family pet. They allow the children to eat until they are satisfied. The pet might be given what is left over. Jesus was in the middle of instructing His disciples. To stop and focus His energy on this woman's request would have taken Him away from His priority at that moment.

There is a wonderful lesson in this text for those of us who struggle to say "No." Did this woman need Jesus' help? Absolutely. Did she have a legitimate need? Yes. But Jesus' priority at that moment was "feeding" His disciples. In a fairly short time, these men would need to be prepared to carry on without Jesus and minister to thousands in His name. Jesus' focus at the time was to instruct and prepare His disciples.

Do you struggle with boundaries and setting priorities? I certainly have struggled in these areas at times. Sometimes it is difficult to say "No," even when we know we should.

> Do you struggle with boundaries and setting priorities?

Is there a task or responsibility you know you should say "No" to at this time? Are you afraid of hurting someone's feelings or leaving people in a bind? Jesus said "No" because He was able to clearly set boundaries based upon His priority at the time. Sometimes, you need to say "No" to one task, in order to be available for some other future responsibility. (Only Christ could remain focused on His priority task and still heal the girl possessed by an evil spirit.)

On the lines below, write a prayer asking God to give you the wisdom you need to set proper limits. Petition Him for the courage to say "Yes" to the areas of service that are a priority for you, and "No" to the areas that would distract you or overload your schedule.

_____

_____

_____

_____

_____

_____

The woman assured Jesus she did not expect Him to take anything away from His disciples. Like a dog eating crumbs dropped by children at a family meal, she believed her daughter could be healed without the slightest interruption or loss by the disciples. She did not consider herself worthy to sit at the table with Jesus, but she was desperate for any crumbs that might be left over. That is faith! Her words indicated a deep belief in His power and authority. "For such a reply" Jesus had compassion on her and granted her request.

What do you learn about the Lord's nature from Psalm 145:8–9?

_____

Jesus is good to all and full of compassion. Let's take a look at a moving example.

Please read Mark 7:31–37.

Notice the gentle approach Jesus took with this man. He was deaf and had a speech impediment, probably the result of his inability to hear. Jesus took him away from the crowd and its distractions so He could communicate with the man through a form of sign language. Jesus enabled this man to exercise the faith needed for his healing. Before we go on, let's look at a couple of instances where faith was required for healing.

Read Matthew 9:27–30 and note what was required for the two blind men to have their sight restored.

_____

_____

Read Luke 8:40–48. In verse 48, what did Jesus say had healed the woman of her bleeding?

_____

_____

Now, re-read Mark 7:33–35 and try to visualize Jesus' actions toward the deaf man.

Jesus put His fingers into the man's ears to draw his attention to them and convey His intention to heal them. Second, Jesus spit (probably on the ground) to indicate a rebuke of that which caused the man's ears to fail. Third, Jesus touched the man's tongue to let him know his speech would also be healed. Jesus then looked up to heaven and commanded that the man's ears be opened and his tongue loosed. Obviously, the man believed Jesus had the power to heal him because he could immediately hear and speak!

> Never let anyone try to convince you our Lord doesn't meet us where we are.

Never let anyone try to convince you our Lord doesn't meet us where we are. Jesus was tender and personal with the man. He didn't simply heal him, He connected with him. He allowed the deaf man to experience his Healer. That is what Christ does for us, too, and it is evidence of His abundant love and overwhelming compassion for each of us. He could work in your life without ever allowing you to know how it happened or by what power. Yet our Lord chooses to reveal Himself. He chooses to make His actions personal. That is healing compassion!

How have you experienced the healing compassion of Jesus in your life? Write your answer and if you are doing this study with a group, be ready to share your answer at your next meeting:

_____

_____

_____

_____

_____

_____

_____

The Bread of Life

I am the living bread that came down from heaven. If anyone eats of this bread, he will live forever. This bread is my flesh, which I will give for the life of the world.

JOHN 6:51

*I*n the next two lessons we will compare the feeding of the five thousand with the feeding of the four thousand to gain a little insight into the lessons Jesus might have been teaching His disciples through His actions. We previously discussed the fact that the loaves were representative of Jesus' flesh broken for the salvation of the world. Today, we will explore additional symbolism contained in the details of these two miraculous events.

Read Mark 8:1–13.

Once again, Jesus displayed His compassion, this time by providing food for the crowd. This miraculous provision is similar to the feeding of the five thousand, with the exception of the number of loaves and the number of people fed, as well as some other interesting distinctions I'd like to point out.

Where does Luke 9:10 tell us the feeding of the five thousand took place?

_____

Now look back at Mark 7:31 from yesterday's text. What region was Jesus in when He healed the deaf and mute man?

_____

The crowd of four thousand gathered somewhere near the Decapolis, a region east of the Jordan River that contained a league of ten cities inhabited by Greeks.[13] Because of the location, this crowd was most likely made up primarily of Gentiles (non-Jews). In contrast, the crowd at Bethsaida would have been primarily Jews. There is some debate about the exact location of the Bethsaida referred to in these passages, but both of the accepted locations were within Jewish territory.

Both miracles reinforce the truth that if we faithfully use the resources we have, God will provide for our needs. In addition, both miraculous feedings were confirmations that Jesus was indeed the long-awaited Messiah and Savior. But the interesting distinctions in locations and details cause me to wonder if the differences were intentional. Perhaps the unique settings symbolized Jesus' intention to bless all nations (Genesis 12:3) and eventually have His disciples carry the gospel to both Jews and Gentiles.

First, let's explore the feeding of the five thousand more closely. Jews were descendants of Abraham and blood heirs to the promises God had made to him. The Jews had been informed continually by God's prophets that a king (or Messiah) would come from Abraham's descendants and would redeem Israel.

According to Isaiah 59:20, who did the prophet say would come?

_____

_____

Redemption means "release or freedom on payment of a price, deliverance by a costly method."[14] The Jews were watching for a Redeemer (Messiah) and were expecting certain things to happen in order to identify Him. One identifying factor was that the Messiah would produce manna from heaven, as God had done in Moses' time. That idea is based upon these words from Moses: "The LORD thy God will raise up unto thee a Prophet from the midst of thee, of thy brethren, like unto me; unto him ye shall hearken" (Deuteronomy 18:15 KJV).

One rabbinical saying that was well-known at the time declared, "As the first redeemer caused the manna to fall from heaven, even so shall the second redeemer cause the manna to fall."[15] The loaves were the bread from heaven the Jews were expecting. Jesus confirmed it when the crowds asked Him for a sign He truly was the awaited Messiah.

Read Jesus' words recorded in John 6:25–31.

> One rabbinical saying that was well-known at the time declared, "As the first redeemer caused the manna to fall from heaven, even so shall the second redeemer cause the manna to fall."

As if providing food for five thousand with five small barley loaves and two small fish wasn't miraculous enough, the people asked for yet another sign. Are you kidding me? I'm amazed by the extreme patience of our Lord—with His people then and, admittedly, with me today. Let's face it, we all struggle with unbelief. Before we take a look at Jesus' response to the skeptical crowd, let's take a trip back to the time of Moses and see what the expectant Jews were talking about.

Please read Exodus 16:13–18.

It was God, not Moses, who provided bread for the Israelites as they wandered in the desert. And it was God in the flesh who provided the bread for the multitudes in our previous reading as well. The religious leaders were so busy measuring miracles that they missed the Bread that should have captured their attention. Let's see what Jesus had to say.

Read John 6:32–51.

Who is the Bread from heaven? _____

Jesus is the Bread of Life and the true Bread from heaven. The bread supplied by God through Moses fed the physical body, but the Bread of Life feeds the Spirit. Jesus Christ is the Word made flesh and He feeds life to our spirits every time we open the Word of God and "chew" on it.

Re-read Mark 6:38–44.

Who actually distributed the bread to the people that day (v. 41)?

_____

_____

According to verse 43, how many baskets were left over?

_____

_____

The Greek word translated "basket" in Mark 6:43 is *kophinos*. It was customary at the time for a Jew to carry a small, pouch-like basket (kophinos) on his belt with a supply of food when traveling. As the disciples gathered the leftover bread that day, each one would have been able to carry a portion of the miraculous bread with him. I imagine that from that day forward, each time he looked at kophinos, he was reminded of Jesus' words, "I am the bread of life" (John 6:35).

Just as the disciples had distributed the miraculous bread to the crowds that day, they were responsible for sharing the Bread of Life with all the Jewish people. In tomorrow's lesson, we will look more closely at the feeding of the four thousand and discover that the apostles were responsible for sharing the Bread of Life with the Gentiles as well as the Jews—as are we.

WEEK THREE   DAY THREE

Receiving Seed

If you belong to Christ, then you are Abraham's seed, and heirs according to the promise.

GALATIANS 3:29

esterday, we discussed the fact that Jesus is the Bread of Life, the true Bread from heaven. The Jews had been waiting for the Messiah to arrive, and providing manna from heaven was one of the signs for which they had been waiting. Because of the region and the particular style of baskets used to distribute the bread to the crowd of five thousand men, we came to the conclusion that the crowd Jesus fed that day were most likely Jews.

In today's lesson, I'd like to focus on the crowd of four thousand who gathered in the Decapolis. As we discussed yesterday, the Decapolis was located in Greek territory, so it is reasonable to assume the crowd was made up primarily of Gentiles. Let's take a little time to reinforce that conclusion.

Re-read Mark 8:1–13. Matthew's account of the event contains a few more clues to the crowd's identity, so please also read Matthew 15:29–32.

What name is used to describe God in verse 31? _____

To the Gentiles, the provision of food would be a demonstration of the power of the God of Israel. Jews, on the other hand, probably would have described the Lord as the God of Abraham, Isaac, and Jacob. The Jews were Israel, so the description of God used by the crowd is a strong indication they were primarily Greeks.

Now interestingly, the baskets that were used to gather the leftovers at this miraculous feeding were different from the kophinos used when Jesus fed the crowd of five thousand. In the original Greek, the word translated "baskets" in Mark 8:8 is *spuris*, "woven reed baskets of various sizes that could be large enough to hold a man."[16]

In fact, Acts 9:23–25 records a time when such a basket did just that.

The basket used by Saul (soon Paul) to escape through an opening in the wall was the same type of basket used to gather leftovers in Mark 8. The Greek word *spuris* is derived from *speiro*, which means "strengthened (through the idea of extending); to scatter, i.e., sow, receive seed."

Interestingly, it is only because of the spiritual transfer of the Seed of Jesus Christ to the Gentiles through their faith in His body broken (like the loaves) that the people in the Decapolis crowd had any spiritual hope. Paul explains the meaning of the term "seed" in his letter to the Galatians. To gain further insight, let's see what Paul had to say.

Please read Galatians 3:15–29.

When non-Jews (Gentiles) believe in Jesus as the Messiah and the Son of God, they become adopted descendants of Abraham. In other words, anyone (not just Jews) who accepts Jesus as Savior becomes a spiritual heir of Abraham and to his Seed, which is Christ.

Jesus talked a lot about seed in His parables. In fact, last week we studied the significance of seedtime and harvest. What is the Seed that is planted in the hearts of people?

_____

_____

_____

Jesus Christ is the Seed, the blessed Word of God. He is our Savior and through Him we have been adopted as children of God.

WEEK THREE

Jesus made it clear that through faith in Him, anyone can be counted as a child of God. Interestingly, when addressing the Jewish religious leaders, Jesus used another vivid illustration to help the proud group understand that God's plan included Gentiles as well as Jews.

> Jesus made it clear that through faith in Him, anyone can be counted as a child of God.

Please read John 10:14–16 and keep in mind, Jesus referred to the Jews as His "sheep."

What insight do you gain from verse 16?

_____

_____

_____

Now read Ephesians 1:4–10.

It was God's plan before the creation of the world for both Jew and Gentile to be brought together into one pasture through Jesus Christ, our Shepherd, and graze together on God's blessed Word—the Bread of Life—broken for us.

Who does John 3:16 indicate will have eternal life?

_____

_____

_____

> I am so thankful Jesus allowed Himself to be nailed to a cross so all sheep could graze on the Word in God's pasture.

I am so thankful Jesus allowed Himself to be nailed to a cross so all sheep could graze on the Word in God's pasture.

Just as the apostles were responsible for carrying the message of redemption to the Jews, they were responsible for extending the Seed of Abraham to the Gentiles. It took some time before the apostles understood, but eventually they got it. As we will see later in our study, it was our friend Peter who was the first to extend the message of salvation through Jesus Christ to the Gentiles.

Most of us fall into the category of Gentiles. As a way of closing today's lesson, write a prayer on the lines below, thanking God for your adoption into His family through Jesus, the Bread of Life, broken for you.

_____

_____

_____

_____

WEEK THREE | DAY FOUR

Clear Vision

"The Spirit of the Lord is on me, because he has anointed me to preach good news to the poor. He has sent me to proclaim freedom for the prisoners and recovery of sight for the blind, to release the oppressed."

LUKE 4:18

*A*fter feeding the four thousand, Jesus and the disciples got back into their boat and sailed to the other side of the lake. They had an interesting discussion during the trip. Let's begin today's lesson by eavesdropping on their conversation.

Read Mark 8:14–21.

The disciples were so focused on bread at this point in their journey that they missed the entire lesson Jesus was trying to teach them. The bread was representative of the Word of God. The events of the preceding few days were not simply lessons about His provision of food for the people.

Read Matthew 16:5–12.

What was Jesus telling the disciples to guard against, according to verse 12?

_____

_____

> The disciples were so focused on bread at this point in their journey that they missed the entire lesson Jesus was trying to teach them.

What additional information do you get about the teaching of the Pharisees from Luke 12:1?

_____

_____

The teaching of the Pharisees and Sadducees was corrupting the Word planted in the hearts of God's people. Even the disciples, who were witnesses to the miracles Jesus performed and walked with Him daily, were susceptible to its corruption.

Yeast causes fermentation in bread. Fermentation is defined as "the decomposition of organic compounds by the action of enzymes."[17] Yeast is a fungus that promotes fermentation, or decomposition, of the natural ingredients in bread. For the Jewish people, unleavened bread was symbolic of purity. The Talmud (the written body of Jewish civil and religious law) says, "Leaven represents the evil impulse of the heart."[18] The disciples should have understood that Jesus was instructing them to be on their guard when it came to the teachings of the Pharisees. The religious leaders' hypocrisy would be like yeast, which would contaminate the purity of Jesus' teachings.

> The Talmud (the written body of Jewish civil and religious law) says, "Leaven represents the evil impulse of the heart."

We also must be careful of false or improper teachings. Regardless of how long we have been believers, we are all vulnerable to false teaching and the confusion it causes unless we continually check against the truth of the Bible what we hear or read. We need to be cautious so we don't fall into the trap of blindly accepting man's word about God's Word.

I encourage you to ask yourself, "Does this line up with the whole counsel of God's Word?" If you are unsure, spend the time necessary to look up passages for yourself. When you read a book that includes Scripture references, look them up in your Bible. Read the paragraph before each passage as well as the paragraph following. Make sure the verse quoted hasn't been taken out of context.

Jesus indicated that the Pharisees were hypocritical. For those of us who are teachers, it is important we do our best to live out what we teach. If we don't, we can do more harm than good. If we live something contrary to what we are teaching, others will notice.

Look back at Mark 8:17–21.

Jesus reminded His disciples of the miracle of the loaves and the significance of the basketfuls left over. However, the disciples still didn't understand.

Read Mark 8:22–26.

Here again Jesus handled the blind man in such a way as to enable him to not only experience healing, but also his Healer. Jesus took the sightless man by the hand, spit on his eyes, enabling him to understand that Jesus intended to heal his sight. Then Jesus touched him and asked the man to respond.

What did the formerly blind man say he saw when he first opened his eyes (v. 24)?

———————————————————————————————————————

Jesus could have restored the man's sight instantly, but instead it was only partially restored. Interestingly, this was quite the object lesson for the disciples. Like the blind man, the perplexed group of followers were unable to see the forest for the trees. They were so focused on the loaves they couldn't seem to grasp the deeper lesson, the big picture. However, with further working of the Master's hands, they too would see with clarity and focus.

Have you ever had an experience where you were so focused on the obvious that you missed the deeper meaning in the situation? If so, give an example.

———————————————————————————————————————

———————————————————————————————————————

Jesus wanted the disciples to understand the deep meaning of the loaves broken for the people. But understanding would come with time and experience. Jesus continually used symbolism to teach His followers.

WEEK THREE

Centuries earlier, the prophet Isaiah spoke about the works of Israel's Messiah. When Jesus began His earthly ministry, He read from the scroll containing that prophecy.

Read Luke 4:14–21.

According to verses 18 and 19, what were some of the acts God had anointed Jesus to perform?

_____

_____

_____

The crux of Jesus' mission was to restore the spiritual sight of the world, enabling them to recognize Him as the Messiah and to accept Him as Savior. The disciples were given much to ponder in the events we studied this week. As we will see in next week's lessons, Peter was paying attention.

> The crux of Jesus' mission was to restore the spiritual sight of the world, enabling them to recognize Him as the Messiah and to accept Him as Savior.

WEEK THREE | DAY FIVE

Personal Application

Application for Day One

We saw Jesus' compassion as He met the needs of two specific individuals: the woman whose child was possessed by a demon and a man crippled by his deaf and mute condition. In each case, it was faith that brought about healing.

Compassion involves feeling grief or pain over another person's suffering with the desire to help. Sometimes in society today, with all its demands and busyness, we can become a bit self-absorbed. In my home town of Houston, Texas, we are so accustomed to seeing homeless people begging along the roads that most of us can drive by without even a twinge of sadness. Our newscasts are full of violence. If we aren't careful, we can harden our hearts to avoid grief or pain. That is necessary to some extent, but have we gone too far? Are we, as a society, losing our sense of compassion for the needs and pain of others?

Jesus continually expressed compassion for the people He encountered.

What does Romans 8:29 tell us?

_____

Compassion involves feeling grief or pain over another person's suffering with the desire to help.

In order to impact our communities for Christ—to be conformed to the likeness of God's Son—we need to express compassion for the people in need around us. We obviously have to exercise discernment when helping a homeless person and we certainly can't cry over every loss or death in our communities, but we can ask God to give us compassion for the people we come in contact with on a daily basis. We can put our arms around a friend who is hurting. We can offer food or clothing to a homeless family on the street. We can listen when a neighbor is experiencing heartache or pain. We can express the compassion of Jesus if we will ask God to make us sensitive to the needs of others.

Application for Day Two

Jesus said whoever eats His flesh and drinks His blood will have eternal life.

Let's read John 6:53–59 again.

As Christians, how do we eat the flesh and drink the blood of Jesus?

_____

We will discuss Communion more thoroughly later in the study as we sit in on the Last Supper with Jesus and His disciples. For now, our focus will be on the words of Jesus in John 6:56. Write that verse here:

_____

_____

_____

_____

_____

Communion is intended to be a physical representation of what is taking place spiritually within the heart of every believer.

Re-read Mark 7:17–23.

In our natural state, our hearts overflow with evil. Our sinful nature is full of evil thoughts. But when Jesus Christ takes up residence within us, we are cleansed and begin to change from the inside out. The blessed Bread of Life takes up residency in our hearts in the form of the Holy Spirit. He fills a hollow, hard heart and begins to change it and mold it into His own likeness. The Seed of Abraham, the Word made flesh, begins to produce fruit according to His kind.

Read Galatians 5:16–23. What is the fruit of the Spirit, according to verses 22 and 23?

_____, _____, _____,

_____, _____, _____,

_____, _____, and _____.

What a contrast to the evil that naturally flows from our hearts! What a difference Jesus Christ makes in a life when He inhabits a heart!

Application for Day Three

When you accepted Jesus Christ as your personal Lord and Savior, you received the spiritual Seed that produces the fruit we read about in the fifth chapter of Galatians.

Look again at the attributes listed as the fruit of the Spirit. In the chart below, indicate the frequency with which you have seen evidence of each aspect of the fruit of the Spirit in your life over the past few months:

	Not at all	On a good day	Frequently	Always
Love				
Joy				
Peace				
Patience				
Kindness				
Goodness				
Faithfulness				
Gentleness				
Self-Control				

Spend a few minutes asking God to manifest more of the fruit of His Spirit in your life. It is only through a relationship with Christ and by prayerfully yielding to the Spirit that you will take on more of these character traits.

The next time you take Communion, understand that Jesus Christ is changing you from the inside out. He is transforming you, day by day, into His likeness and into the person that God designed you to become.

When Jesus said we must eat His flesh, He meant far more than just eating a cracker or piece of bread on Sunday morning. We are called to consume and incorporate His way of thinking into our own lives. Likewise, when He said we must drink His blood, He intended for us to take on His sacrificial lifestyle and allow Him to become our source of life.

Application for Day Four

Jesus said the teaching of the Pharisees was like yeast that would spread and contaminate the purity of the Word of God in people's hearts.

Has there been a time when you were deceived by teaching that did not line up with the full counsel of God's Word? I think of the "health and wealth gospel" (also called the "prosperity gospel") that teaches people to believe that if they live in obedience to God and do everything correctly, they will live in complete health and will receive abundant monetary blessings from God. I agree that God wants us to live victoriously on this earth, but when I study all that Scripture teaches about money, I don't find support for the teaching that God promises His people will be healthy, wealthy, and wise.

> Has there been a time when you were deceived by teaching that did not line up with the full counsel of God's Word?

The "whole counsel of God's Word" is a term that means to see what is said throughout all of Scripture on a particular subject. Many times, we take a single verse out of context and think we understand what the passage means. However, other passages, read alone, might indicate something different. The best method I know of to fully grasp what Scripture teaches about a particular issue is to look up every passage on that subject. Once I've studied every verse and its context, I have a better grasp of what God has to say about the matter.

Third John 2 is a verse I hear quoted often to back up the idea we are promised health and wealth if we are living in accordance with God's Word. I hear the verse quoted most often from the King James Version: "Beloved, I wish above all things that you mayest prosper and be in health, even as thy soul prospereth."

The Greek word translated "health" in this verse is *hugiaino*, which means "to have sound health; i.e., to be well (in body); to be uncorrupt (true in doctrine); to be safe and sound, to be whole." The word can mean to be well in body, but it can also mean to be true in doctrine. So what did John mean? The answer can be found by reading the remainder of the paragraph in which the verse is found.

Read 3 John 2–4.

These passages talk about walking in the truth. They don't talk about how physically healthy these brothers were, but how sound their doctrine was and how they had been, remaining true to godly principles. In context, verse 2 doesn't seem to support the teaching that God promises physical health to the righteous this side of heaven.

I hope you will "watch out for the yeast of the Pharisees" (Mark 8:15) and be on guard for false or improper teachings.

Read John 8:31–32.

What will set you free? _____

_____

Let's watch our doctrine closely and be diligent in our pursuit of truth.

Week 4

Humbling Encounters

Rocky Revelation

Then shalt thou walk in thy way safely, and thy foot shall not stumble.

PROVERBS 3:23 KJV

*I*n our lessons last week, by providing Bread from heaven on two occasions Jesus revealed for the masses He was the long-awaited Messiah. He also issued a stern warning to the disciples, urging them to guard against the Pharisees' and Saducees' false or improper teachings.

Peter was paying attention. Let's see what he learned. Please read Mark 8:27–30.

Who did Peter say Jesus was? _____

Peter was starting to understand. Jesus was the Messiah! As we will see in our next reading, Jesus was quite pleased with Peter's revelation.

Read Matthew 16:13–20.

According to verse 17, who revealed the identity of Jesus to Peter?

_____

God gave Peter insight into the full identity of Jesus. And through Jesus, God also gave Peter insight into his own identity. As we discussed in Week One, the name Peter means "rock." In verse 18, Jesus made a distinction between Peter and the "rock" upon which He would build His church. The Greek word used for Peter in this verse is *petros* and it means, "a piece of rock, larger than a stone." However, the word translated "rock" in the same passage is *petra*. It is the same as *petros* but refers to a mass of rock. In other words, Peter was just a piece of the mass of rock upon which Jesus would build His church.

Let's look at another time in Scripture when Jesus referred to a *petra*, or "mass of rock."

Please read Matthew 7:24–27.

What does a wise man build his house upon?_____

Romans 9:33 in the King James Version reads, "As it is written, Behold, I lay in Sion a stumblingstone and a rock of offence: and whosoever believeth on him shall not be ashamed."

Now read Ephesians 2:19–21.

Jesus builds His church on the foundation of pieces of rock brought together with Him to make a mass of rock. The apostles and prophets were the foundation, with Jesus Christ as the cornerstone. A cornerstone joins together an entire building and strengthens it.

In Christ we are all part of God's holy church. Look back at Matthew 16:18.

What do you think Jesus meant when He said the gates of Hades will not overcome His church?

_____

_____

In the Hebrew culture, the term "gates of Hades" represented the place where all dead went.[19] Jesus was making one of His first references to His impending death on the cross. Although His physical body would endure death, the gates of Hades would not be able to hold Him. He and His spiritual body (the church) would overcome death.

> In the Hebrew culture, the term "gates of Hades" represented the place where all dead went.

Now, Jesus made another seemingly strange statement to Peter. Re-read Matthew 16:19.

This phrase is based on an Old Testament prophecy of Isaiah. Read Isaiah 22:20–22 and note what responsibility Eliakim was given:

_____

The duty of Eliakim was to be a faithful steward of the house of David. "So then what Jesus was saying to Peter is that in the days to come, he would be the steward of the Kingdom. And in the case of Peter the whole idea is that of opening, not shutting the door of the Kingdom."[20]

What further insight do you gain from Revelation 3:7?

_____

_____

Jesus possesses the keys to the kingdom of heaven. Peter was the first to recognize Him as the Christ (Messiah) and the Son of God. And Peter, the *petros,* would have the primary responsibility of being a steward of that kingdom, opening the gates as he began creating the *petra,* the mass of rock which would become the church.

Interestingly, Jesus possesses another key. According to Revelation 1:18, what key is that?

_____

_____

Jesus holds the keys to both eternal life and eternal death. He is the Lord over all Creation. And one day, every knee shall bow and every tongue will confess that He is Lord to the glory of the heavenly Father.

Jesus was beginning to reveal to the apostles the plan of salvation through His death on the cross! He continued with that theme in our next reading.

Read Mark 8:31–9:1.

Peter wanted to protect His Lord. He was a passionate and courageous man with strong emotions. At that moment, I truly believe Peter would have given his life to protect Jesus. What he failed to understand was that Jesus would willingly lay *His* life down—not only for Peter, but for the entire world.

Jesus rebuked Peter because Peter's thoughts were in direct opposition to the will of God. To Jesus' question, "Who do you say I am?" Peter had said, "You are the Christ." Yet he was attempting to reduce Jesus to the level of men, contradicting the very statements he'd made so boldly just moments before.

I relate well to Peter. One moment I can passionately tell others of Jesus' power and authority over every circumstance. Then, minutes later, I'm confronted by my own lack of faith as I try to take matters into my own hands.

As we continue our study, we will see more of Peter's internal struggles to grasp the magnitude of Christ's power and love. To conclude our lesson for today, reflect on the struggles you have dealt with over the last month. What have your responses revealed about your faith?

_____

_____

> Peter had to learn to trust Jesus and not rely upon his own limited understanding of the events that would soon unfold before him.

Based on your actions, do you believe you would hear words of praise or words of rebuke from the Lord?

_____

_____

I find it incredibly encouraging to know Peter heard both!

Peter had a revelation about Jesus' identity as the Christ and he enjoyed a moment of commendation from his Lord. But like a man walking barefoot over rocky terrain, Peter wavered and stumbled over his fresh revelation.

Read Proverbs 3:5–6.

Peter had difficulty with the bitter reality of certain aspects of his revelation that "Jesus is the Christ!" Jesus would suffer greatly. Peter had to learn to trust Jesus and not rely upon his own limited understanding of the events that would soon unfold before him.

Mountainous Lessons

Then a cloud appeared and enveloped them, and a voice came from the cloud:
"This is my Son, whom I love. Listen to Him!"

MARK 9:7

Today we will tag along with Peter as he traveled with Jesus to a mountaintop. There Peter will learn some of the most important lessons of his life. Frankly, they are some of the most important lessons of our lives as well.

To begin, please read Mark 9:2–8.

This is believed to be one of Peter's sermons, translated and recorded by Mark. James and John were left speechless by the glorious images before them. Peter "did not know what to say" (v. 6), yet you'll notice that didn't stop him from speaking anyway.

Let's read Matthew's account of this incident. He gives a few additional details.

Please read Matthew 17:1–5.

What was Peter doing when the bright cloud enveloped them and a voice spoke from the cloud?

_____

High on that mountain, God allowed Peter, James, and John to become eyewitnesses to the majesty (power and splendor) of Jesus. Unfortunately, Peter's focus on preserving the moment nearly caused him to miss the entire point of the images before him. He chattered like a magpie in a moment when he should have silently fallen to his knees with a sense of awe and reverence.

Did you notice that God interrupted Peter as he rambled on? God spoke, confirming for Peter, James, and John that Jesus was not only the long-awaited Messiah, but His beloved Son. Peter had been reprimanded by Jesus for his outbursts before, but this rebuke clearly came from the Father: "Listen to Him!"

Read Matthew 17:6–13.

According to verse 6, how did the disciples react to God's reprimand?

_____

There's the posture God was looking for!

When did Jesus indicate that the disciples could tell others what had happened on the mountain?

_____

High on that mountain, God allowed Peter, James, and John to become eyewitnesses to the majesty (power and splendor) of Jesus. Unfortunately, Peter's focus on preserving the moment nearly caused him to miss the entire point of the images before him.

Once again we find Jesus preparing the disciples for His death and resurrection. They had seen Jesus in His glorified state. That glimpse of the majesty of Christ would help the awestruck men reconcile and understand the events soon to unfold. As they came down from that mountaintop experience with Jesus, the three privileged disciples were immediately brought back to the reality of the world around them.

Read Mark 9:14–29.

The other disciples were arguing with the teachers of the law because they were unable to drive out the evil spirit from the boy. Why do you think this would cause an argument?

_____

_____

The teachers of the law used this incident to question the validity of Jesus and the authority He granted to the disciples. Can't you hear them? "These are followers of that Jesus. See, they have no power to drive out demons. This Jesus is a fraud!"

Once again we find Jesus preparing the disciples for His death and resurrection.

We don't know the details of the argument, but I imagine it must have gone something like that, for Jesus certainly gave the crowd a strong rebuke. "O unbelieving generation, how long shall I stay with you? How long shall I put up with you?"

Humiliated, the disciples asked Jesus later why they had been unable to drive out the spirit. What was Jesus' response in Mark 9:29?

_____

The disciples had been trying to act in their own power. How often do we do the very same thing? We try our best to handle circumstances in our strength. We expend large amounts of energy. We get frustrated and exhausted. Then, humiliated, we seek the Lord for guidance. To operate with the full power and authority intended we need to pray first, then act.

Read James 5:13–16.

Prayer is powerful and effective. Regardless of what trials you face, it is prayer that moves you forward in God's will and His grace. Through prayer, God will guide you through your circumstances and enable you to accomplish far more than you could ever accomplish on your own.

What about you? Are you currently facing challenges that you have been trying to solve in your own power or with your own methods? Please briefly tell about them:

_____

_____

Read Mark 9:30–32.

According to these verses, what was the main topic of study for the day?

_____

Peter, James, and John had been eyewitnesses to the majesty of Jesus as He was transfigured alongside Moses and Elijah. They'd seen Him reprimand the people and even issue a rebuke at the skeptical, cynical attitudes of the teachers of the law. The disciples also had seen Jesus show tremendous compassion toward a man struggling to believe that his son could really be healed.

> Peter, James, and John had been eyewitnesses to the majesty of Jesus as He was transfigured alongside Moses and Elijah.

Yet Jesus talked of being betrayed and killed, then rising from the dead. The disciples could not assimilate the information. They had difficulty reconciling what they had experienced to the events Jesus foretold. This time, even Peter kept silent.

Perhaps God's words, "Listen to Him!" were still ringing in his ears. Peter needed to listen. For nothing could prepare the disciples for the events that would soon take place. Jesus knew the disciples did not understand, but He also knew that His teaching would mold and define their faith.

Jesus is the Son of God. All things are possible for him who believes. The Son of Man must die for the sins of the world. Ah, but if they were listening carefully, they also heard that after three days He would rise!

Mountainous lessons indeed.

WEEK FOUR | DAY THREE

Humbled Servants

"For everyone who exalts himself will be humbled, and he who humbles himself will be exalted."

LUKE 14:11

*T*oday we will witness a lesson in humility. More often than not, my own lessons in humility have come from strong doses of humiliation. May today be one of those times when we learn from the mistakes of others.

Read Mark 9:33–37.

What were the disciples arguing about on the road?

What must we do to be considered great by Jesus' standards? (v. 35)

To illustrate being a true servant of all, Jesus took a little child in His arms. Children in that culture were considered the least significant members of society, so this illustration not only told the disciples to serve those in lower positions, but also to welcome them and accept them. It appears the disciple John was feeling a bit convicted, for he made an appropriate confession in our next reading.

Please read Mark 9:38–41.

Why had the disciples instructed the man to stop driving out demons?

Just because this man was not one of the Twelve was insufficient cause for them to stop him. Could it be that the disciples were a bit jealous?

Look back at Mark 9:17–18. What had the disciples been unable to do?

The disciples may have been just a bit humiliated by this man, whom they considered to be of a lower position, showing them up. They were concerned with preserving their own positions. Again, Jesus put the emphasis on service, not position.

Read Luke 14:1–11.

God often uses humiliation to bring about a deeper level of humility in us. The disciples were setting themselves up to be humbled as they sought to be the greatest. Peter, James, and John had accompanied Jesus to the mountain and witnessed His majesty at the Transfiguration. I can't help but believe that at least some of the three privileged disciples were the instigators of the argument over position. I'm not sure Peter would have presumptuously sat in one of the places of honor, but James and John? Well, let's take a peek ahead for a moment.

> God often uses humiliation to bring about a deeper level of humility in us.

Read Mark 10:35–45.

Peter probably wouldn't have considered himself the greatest, but I can guess he was indignant that James and John tried to claim those positions. Knowing Peter, he was probably the first to speak up and make his feelings known!

What does Luke 14:11 tell us will happen to the individual who exalts himself?

_____

Has there been a time in your life when God used humiliation to bring you a greater level of humility? If so, describe the circumstances:

_____

_____

_____

_____

Our next few points may make you a bit uncomfortable. But let's ask God to cultivate a greater sense of humility in our hearts as we continue this lesson.

In Mark 9:42, Jesus said it would be better for a person to be thrown into the sea with a large millstone tied around his neck than to what?

_____

_____

The Greek word translated "to sin" in the New International Version of Mark 9:42 is *skandalizo*, from which we get the word "scandalize." It means, "to entrap; trip up (stumble) or entice to sin, apostasy, or displeasure, to offend." Basically, Jesus indicated that if someone enticed a child (or someone immature in the faith) to sin, it would be better to be drowned in the sea than to receive the punishment and wrath of God.

Can you think of some actions that might entice children or new believers to sin?

_____

_____

Even the most mature Christians can behave in a way that negatively impacts others. Write 1 Corinthians 8:9 in your own words:

_____

_____

_____

Even the most mature Christians can behave in a way that negatively impacts others.

We need to live out to the best of our ability what we say we believe. A few years ago, a good friend of mine was put in a situation quite common for business owners. She and her husband owned their own business and were making some improvements to their home. When preparing the invoice, the contractor suggested she and her husband pay with a company check so they could take a tax deduction for the work. But the work was being done at their residence, not their business. Stunned, my friend did not respond. Later, she simply sent a check from their personal account and graciously thanked the contractor for a job well done. She was not willing to compromise her principles or taint her testimony. Most of all, she desired to please God. That kind of integrity keeps us from "becoming a stumbling block to the weak," or causing an immature believer to sin. My friend and her husband took seriously their commitment to be witnesses for Christ.

Read Mark 9:43–50.

Anything that causes us to be tempted to sin, especially if it affects others, needs to be eliminated from our lives. Why do you think that requires humility?

_____

_____

_____

Jesus ends this teaching by reminding everyone to "be at peace with each other." Let's see what our friend Peter had to say on the subject of being at peace with others.

Please read 1 Peter 3:8–17.

Peter urges us to be humble and compassionate. That behavior will help us be at peace with people around us. He also encouraged us to strive to do what is right—always.

Sometimes that is difficult. But even if we suffer negative results or persecution for our "good" behavior, Peter tells us to repay evil with blessing so that we too will be blessed. That's a lofty goal. But if we bless those who persecute us, Peter says those who speak maliciously against us will be ashamed of their slander.

> Peter urges us to be humble and compassionate. That behavior will help us be at peace with people around us.

Peacemakers are not quick to judge or hasty to correct. Peacemakers unify and put others first. It takes true humility to bless those who persecute us. And I'm sure the disciples struggled with it, just as we do. For the disciples to be at peace with the people around them, they needed to focus on serving others, even those they considered to be of low position. Sounds like a lesson in humility, don't you think?

WEEK FOUR | DAY FOUR

Along the Road

Jesus then left that place and went into the region of Judea and across the Jordan. Again crowds of people came to him, and as was his custom, he taught them.

MARK 10:1

Today we will walk with Peter and the other disciples along a dusty dirt road with Jesus. "As was His custom," Jesus taught many along the way.

To begin our journey, read Mark 10:1–12.

Jesus referred back to Creation, when God created man and woman. God never intended for people to divorce. When we marry, we become something entirely new together, both physically and spiritually—one flesh.

What did the Pharisees point out that Moses permitted, according to verse 4?

_____

_____

Let's see what Moses actually said. Please read Deuteronomy 24:1–4.

The purpose of Moses' words is found in verse 4. The Israelites were divorcing their wives. Moses was simply setting guidelines for remarriage because the people were already doing it. As Jesus said, "Their hearts were hard," and that is why the subject had to be addressed in the first place. Jesus made it clear that God desires for husbands and wives to remain committed to their marriages and to one another.

Perhaps as you read this lesson, you feel your marriage is hopeless. Maybe the last thing you want to read is that God desires for you to remain married. Please know that I do not advocate abuse, and I recognize there are certain situations where divorce is unavoidable, but I also believe there is always hope through Christ. If you are struggling in your marriage, I urge you to seek out your pastor or find a good Christian counselor and get some sound, godly guidance. Pray daily for God to restore your marriage. For "all things are possible with God" (Mark 10:27).

> If you are struggling in your marriage, I urge you to seek out your pastor or find a good Christian counselor and get some sound, godly guidance.

The Pharisees were incorrect in their understanding of the law regarding divorce. Jesus corrected them and made many other adjustments to the doctrine of the people as He traveled along the road.

Please read Mark 10:13–16.

Why do you think Jesus was "indignant" at the disciples' behavior?

_____

_____

_____

Look back at Mark 9:36–37. What did Jesus say the disciples were doing when they welcomed children in His name?

Again, what had the topic of discussion been among the disciples as they walked along the road, according to Mark 9:33–34?

These twelve men still didn't get seem to get it. They were so focused on their own positions and importance that they failed to understand that these "little ones" possessed the innocence and humility required to accept Jesus with total trust. Jesus was tender and sweet to the children. Clearly, they were precious to Him. As God's children, each of us is also important to our Savior. He loves us, and Jesus wants us to trust Him with our whole hearts. But in order for us to allow God's complete spiritual rule in our lives, we must humble ourselves and trust Him as children do.

My son, Brandon, had an EEG when he was about four years old. I will never forget the drive to the hospital for the test. He asked many questions. I assured him the test wouldn't hurt, but explained that he would have to lie still for a very long time (a monumental request of my active and fidgety four-year-old boy). He held my hand tightly as we walked into the hospital and made our way to the testing location.

When we entered the room, Brandon's eyes opened wide as he looked at all the equipment and the wires that would soon be attached to his little golden blonde head. He looked up at me with those dark brown eyes, attempting to hold back tears. The wise technician quickly began to explain the process. After she assured that it wouldn't hurt, he looked at me with wrinkled brow and said, "I will do it if you tell me a story, Mommy." I agreed. With courageous determination he got up onto the table and stiffly, but submissively, lay back on the pillow. He trusted. He accepted what the technician had said without analyzing or arguing. He chose to believe she was telling him the truth. As I told a lengthy story about an adventuresome frog, my brave son stayed just as still as a four-year-old little boy could be. As I watched him, I wondered how often I had failed to submissively be still and trust God. Child-like trust . . . that is what Jesus is looking for.

Although Jesus had just taught the disciples that the "kingdom of God belongs to such as these," they were scolding the people for bringing their children to Him. But once again, Jesus revealed His love and compassion for children.

What does Mark 10:16 say Jesus did?

> If you are a parent, when was the last time you took your children in your arms and blessed them with words of praise? Children respond to praise like flowers respond to water.

WEEK FOUR

_____

_____

The Greek word translated "blessed" in this verse is *eulogeo,* which means "to speak well of, to invoke divine favor upon, bless, praise." To emphasize His point, Jesus took the children in His arms and spoke words of praise to them.

If you are a parent, when was the last time you took your children in your arms and blessed them with words of praise? Children respond to praise like flowers respond to water. Whether you "watered" your children with praise yesterday or last month, make a point to follow Jesus' example and bless your children today. Some of that blessing just might splash over on you as well!

For our final passage today, please read Mark 10:17–31.

Why do you think the wealthy man was unwilling to sell what he had and follow Jesus?

_____

_____

_____

The key is probably in verse 24. Some manuscripts read, "The disciples were amazed at his words. But Jesus said again, "Children, how hard it is for those who trust in riches to enter the kingdom of God!"

The rich man not only possessed wealth, but evidently the wealth possessed him. He trusted in it. He was unwilling to give up the things he had for the eternal life he said he wanted. Had he been completely honest, he would have probably phrased his question, "What must I do to continue living in my comfort and privilege for all time?"

What did Jesus tell the disciples in Luke 9:24–25?

_____

_____

_____

What did Peter say to Jesus in Mark 10:28?

_____

_____

Isn't it just like Peter to make sure Jesus noticed? Peter was passionate about following Jesus. He had given up everything he had to follow his Master. Jesus had seen Peter as the "Rock" and had changed everything about his life. Peter had chosen to follow Jesus and was being transformed into the man Jesus knew he could become.

Jesus also knew who the wealthy man had the potential to become. If only he had taken his focus off his wealth, given generously to others, and followed Jesus, the man might have had a major impact on the world for Christ.

> May we never allow the comforts of this world to keep us from becoming the women God truly intends for us to be!

May we never allow the comforts of this world to keep us from becoming the women God truly intends for us to be! It may require sacrifice, but there is no sacrifice we can ever make that would surpass the sacrifice Jesus made on the cross—for you and for me. As with the wealthy young man, Jesus looks at each of us and loves us. What He asks of us is only that which will enable us to attain our full potential.

Personal Application

On Day One we read that Peter had difficulty accepting the fresh revelation God gave him regarding his Companion and Lord. How could it be possible the long-awaited Savior of the world would be killed? Then on Day Two we traveled to a mountaintop with Peter and witnessed the majesty of Jesus as he was transfigured. We were also given additional information about Jesus' approaching death and resurrection. On Day Three Peter and the other disciples were humbled as Jesus taught them they must possess the trust and humility of a child in order to be used greatly for God's purposes. And finally, on Day Four we learned many lessons about the interpretation of God's law.

Each lesson challenged ideals the disciples had grown up with and held their entire lives.

Read Mark 10:32–34.

According to verse 32, how did the disciples react to Jesus' statements about His death?

_____

_____

Peter and the disciples were amazed by the information Jesus was giving them. Spit on? Flogged? Rising from the dead? How could this be? To forge ahead in God's will, the disciples had to trust more than ever. That trust would come from the relationship each of them had with Jesus.

Write out Proverbs 3:5–6 in your own words:

_____

_____

_____

The Hebrew word translated "acknowledge" in this verse is *yada,* which means "to know." The disciples knew Jesus because they had spent time with Him, listened to Him, and learned from Him. This time, Peter did not take Jesus aside and rebuke Him. He didn't try to stop Him. He was beginning to trust that Jesus had a higher purpose in what He was saying.

Peter had revealed a lack of trust in Jesus when he took Him aside and rebuked Him. Peter didn't like what Jesus had said and he decided to try to take control.

But don't we often do the same thing? When we don't like what God is doing in our lives, we resist, we look for another direction, we question. Sometimes we even take the Creator of the universe aside and tell Him that "this shall never happen!"

> Learning to "lean not on your own understanding" (Proverbs 3:5) comes through a relationship with your Savior, just as it did for the disciples.

Learning to "lean not on your own understanding" (Proverbs 3:5) comes through a relationship with your Savior, just as it did for the disciples. We get to know Him through God's Word, by witnessing His activity, and by talking to Him on a regular basis through prayer. The better we "know" Him, the more we are able to trust Him, regardless of what trials or situations we face.

Read John 14:1–10.

What insight do you gain into the identity of Jesus?

_____

_____

_____

_____

Rather than focusing on the application for each day individually, this week we will spend the rest of this lesson nailing down our concept of three attributes of God: His omnipotence, His omnipresence, and His omniscience. By studying these attributes, we will increase our ability to trust God in circumstances where we are required to "lean not on our own understanding."

Let's begin with God's omnipotence. Omnipotence is God's ability to do whatever He wills. Read the following Scripture verses and in your own words write what you learn about God's omnipotence:

Jeremiah 32:17 _____

Matthew 19:26 _____

God is not limited in what He can do. Spend a few moments in prayer and ask Him to reveal any areas of your life where you have lacked trust in His ability to work on your behalf. If a situation comes to mind, please describe it:

> God is not limited by time or space. The fullness of our heavenly Father is present everywhere, all the time.

_____

_____

_____

WEEK FOUR

Now let's explore what is meant by God's omnipresence. Basically, the term means that God is present everywhere. Read the following Scripture passages and write in your own words what you have learned about God's omnipresence:

Psalm 139:7–10: _____

Proverbs 15:3: _____

God is not limited by time or space. The fullness of our heavenly Father is present everywhere, all the time. God is in your home, your workplace, wherever you may be, but most importantly, His Holy Spirit resides *within* your very being.

There is no place on Earth where you are out of His reach. I find that incredibly encouraging, don't you? Nothing is hidden. Spend a few minutes in prayer and ask God to reveal any area of your life that you may have been attempting to hide from Him. This could be sin, something that has hurt you, or even a wrong attitude toward another person. If anything comes to mind, please write it down:

_____

_____

_____

_____

_____

Finally, let's analyze God's omniscience. Our God has perfect knowledge of all things past, present, and future. He has the ability to know exactly how to accomplish His purposes. Read the following Scripture passages and in your own words write what you learn about God's omniscience:

Psalm 139:1–4 _____

Psalm 147:5 _____

Have you ever tried to put a time limit on God? I know I have. We figure if He hasn't moved in a way we expect within a certain period of time, then we're on our own. Have you ever figured God was too busy handling "bigger" problems to deal with the situations going on in your life? The truth is, He knows everything you are dealing with

> Have you ever tried to put a time limit on God?

and He cares about the smallest details of your circumstances. Many times, He is working in the small details every day, but we get so focused on seeing Him do something "amazing" that we miss the subtle activity of God.

When my son, Brandon, was in middle school, he had a strong desire to be accepted by his peers. From my perspective, he didn't seem to be open enough about his Christianity. We had numerous discussions about his need for acceptance and I diligently prayed that God would give him the courage to share his faith with friends. I was agonizing over the struggle I could see taking place within him. I kept expecting him to wear a Christian T-shirt to school or to play Christian music when his friends were over. But he resisted my suggestions and I sensed the Spirit of God nudging me to give him space and stop pushing my agenda.

One day as I was carpooling Brandon and two of his friends to our church's monthly middle school fellowship and dance, I realized Brandon had invited a friend to attend the event with him almost every month. He had been sharing his faith with friends. It wasn't in the bold way I had been suggesting, but in a manner he found comfortable. Conviction washed over me as I realized I had been so determined to pressure him into sharing his faith in a way I would, I didn't even recognize I had been carpooling the answer to my prayers to church every month.

Take a moment to ask God to open your eyes to His activity in your life, especially the subtle, daily ways He works on your behalf and provides for your needs. Who knows? You just might discover that you have been carpooling a few answered prayers yourself.

Week 5

The Time Approaches

Cloaks Surrendered

Throwing his cloak aside, he jumped to his feet and came to Jesus.

MARK 10:50

To begin our study this week, we will join a triumphal procession as Jesus enters the gates of Jerusalem.

Please read Mark 10:46–52.

Jesus was on His way to Jerusalem for the Passover. Jewish men over the age of twelve living within fifteen miles of Jerusalem were required by law to make their way there for the Passover celebration. As a result, there would have been many people on the road that day. Most likely, Bartimaeus's begging had proved lucrative.

What was Bartimaeus's reaction when Jesus called him (v. 50)?

In Jesus' day, a cloak was usually one's most valuable possession. "It was used as a blanket, a sack to carry things, a place to sit, a pledge for debt, and, of course, clothing."[21] Bartimaeus probably collected his entire day's earnings in his cloak. Yet when Jesus called him, he threw the cloak (quite possibly his *only* possession) aside, along with any money he'd received, and jumped to his feet.

How did Bartimaeus address Jesus in verses 47 and 48?

_____

What did Bartimaeus say he wanted (v. 51)? _____

Bartimaeus already had far more spiritual sight than most Jews. "Son of David" was a term reserved only for the Messiah. Bartimaeus recognized Jesus as the Messiah and believed in His ability to heal. The blind beggar set an example for all who place their faith in Jesus Christ. He threw aside his earthly possessions, jumped to his feet, and "came to Jesus." How often we come to Him still tightly holding our "cloaks" in our hands!

Please read Mark 11:1–8.

What did the two disciples throw upon the back of the colt?

_____

The two disciples surrendered their cloaks, and many others began to spread their cloaks along the road before Jesus. They were giving Jesus a king's welcome.

Read an excerpt from the anointing of one of Israel's kings, Jehu, in 2 Kings 9:11–13. What did the officers do to acknowledge Jehu as king in verse 13?

_____

_____

Now read Zechariah 9:9–10, which is a prophecy about the Messiah. Upon what does the Messiah ride into Jerusalem, according to verse 9?

_____

As the people surrendered their cloaks, they were acknowledging Jesus as their long-awaited king. The cloaks laid upon the dusty entrance to Jerusalem that day would have been of various fabrics and forms. The wealthy sometimes had cloaks made from colorful silk with wide sleeves. The poor, on the other hand, often had cloaks made of thick wool with slits for the arms. The cloaks represented each person's status (great or meager), and determined their comfort and their protection. Regardless of the fabric or style, the people willingly laid their most valuable possession before their king.

What "cloak" do you need to surrender at the feet of Jesus today? Is it your position? Your wealth? Perhaps it's your comfort or protection. Is there anything you are wrapping around yourself like a cloak of security? If so, write a prayer of surrender:

> What "cloak" do you need to surrender at the feet of Jesus today?

_____

_____

_____

_____

Now read Mark 11:9–11.

"Hosanna" is a Hebrew expression that originally was a prayer to God meaning, "O save us now!"[22] The crowd was enthusiastically quoting a familiar psalm traditionally sung at the closing of the Passover meal. Jesus was being ushered into Jerusalem with a king's welcome. The Messiah had finally come!

According to John 12:13, what kind of branches were the people waving and laying before Jesus?

_____

At another annual Jewish feast, the Feast of Tabernacles, God's people would listen as a choir sang the Hallel, which is Psalms 113–118. At the proper time in the song, the people would waive their palm branches and join in singing Psalm 118:25–26 as the priests marched around the altar.[23]

Read Psalm 118:25–26. What is the focus of these verses?

_____

This celebration was in anticipation of the long-awaited Messiah and Savior.

It is clear that as the people surrendered their cloaks before Jesus and waived their palm branches, they were joyfully acknowledging Jesus as their King and Messiah. They were anticipating salvation for the Jewish people. It truly was a triumphal entry!

As a way of closing, read Revelation 7:9.

One day, my sister in Christ, you will surrender your earthly cloak of a body and slip into a white robe of righteousness. You will waive a palm branch before your Savior and King and make a triumphal entry with Him into eternal life!

> *Give thanks to the LORD, for he is good; his love endures forever.*
>
> PSALM 118:29

WEEK FIVE DAY TWO

Withered State

Peter remembered and said to Jesus, "Rabbi, look! The fig tree you cursed has withered!"

MARK 11:21

Yesterday we witnessed Jesus' triumphal entry into Jerusalem amid waiving palm branches and surrendered cloaks. Today, we will once again walk with Jesus through Jerusalem's gates. This time, Jesus attracts attention of a different sort. As we will see, the King of kings and Lord of lords turns the tables on His disciples' enthusiasm.

Read Mark 11:12–19.

What was Jesus looking for on the fig tree? _____

"In Palestine fig trees produced crops of small edible buds in March, followed by the appearance of large green leaves in early April. These buds were common food for local peasants."[24] It was the Passover season, which falls around the middle of April, so Jesus was expecting to find buds on the fig tree. The actual figs were usually produced sometime around June. That's why we're told it was not the season for figs.

I'd like to suggest that this barren fig tree represented the state of the Jewish people at the time.

According to Hosea 9:10, what does God say it was like for Him when He saw Israel's fathers or ancestors?

_____

_____

What did God say about fig trees through the prophet in Jeremiah 8:11–13?

_____

_____

The fig tree Jesus encountered was described as being "in leaf." So like the religious leaders and the nation of Israel as a whole, the tree appeared to be healthy from a distance. But upon closer inspection, like the Jewish people, the tree was fruitless. The people had the appearance of spirituality, but their hearts were barren and their motives were impure.

In Mark 11:17, Jesus said the people had turned God's temple into a "den of robbers." To gain a better understanding of Jesus' words, read Jeremiah 7:1–2, 9–11.

What insight do you gain regarding God's feelings toward the activities we perform in a place of worship?

_____

_____

_____

Jesus was not just upset over the actions taking place in the temple that day. He was angry over the entire lifestyle of the Jewish religious leaders. They were full of hypocrisy. At the temple, they put on the outward appearance of devotion to God, but their hearts were far from Him. The chief priests and teachers of the law knew exactly what Jesus meant, and they were furious.

Read Mark 11:20–25.

Did you notice Peter's particular choice of words? The fig tree had "withered." Peter understood that the fig tree represented the Jewish people. I just wonder if his heart sank into his stomach as he recalled Jesus' words of the prior day: "May no one ever eat fruit from you again." But what does Jesus tell Peter to do?

_____

The Jewish people were awaiting a king and savior. Jesus had made it very clear to the disciples He was that king. Peter had even said it himself—"You are the Christ." Yet here, Jesus symbolically cursed His people. How could they be saved?! Certainly this disturbed Peter greatly. Yet Jesus tells him, "Have faith in God" and trust that God can move the obstacles of unbelief and legalism and hypocrisy to save His people.

> The Jewish people were awaiting a king and savior. Jesus had made it very clear to the disciples He was that king.

Look again at Mark 11:17. What does Jesus say the temple should be?

_____

Jesus was calling Peter to pray. The mountainous obstacles could be cast into the sea, but the people were in need of prayer.

Let's take a look at some of Jesus' instructions regarding prayer.

Read Matthew 6:5–15.

Peter needed to let go of the bitterness or resentment he held for his people and forgive so he too could be forgiven and effectively intercede for them. The fig tree was a visual representation of the fate of the Jewish people without intervention from God. Peter was commissioned to pray for just that intervention. Let's see what happened next.

Read Mark 11:27–33.

This time, the chief priests and the teachers of the law brought along the leaders, who governed the community, as they confronted Jesus.

Whom did the religious leaders fear, according to verse 32?

_____

_____

They brought the elders along, hoping to apply added pressure to Jesus and stop Him from disrupting the activities in the temple courts. But Jesus turned the tables on them. He used the elders' presence to His own advantage. Like self-absorbed politicians, the elders were unwilling to answer His questions in front of the people.

I am constantly astounded by the shrewdness of Jesus. Every detail of His life was a lesson for the disciples (and for us as well!). When Jesus sent the twelve apostles out for the first time on their own, He gave them some specific instructions. What were those instructions, according to Matthew 10:16?

_____

_____

Jesus led by example. He was "shrewd as [a snake] and innocent as [a dove]. The religious leaders were plotting to kill Jesus, and we will see they ultimately succeeded. However, Jesus controlled the moment it would happen.

Tomorrow we will witness numerous attempts by the religious leaders to find a reason to arrest Jesus. But the appointed time had not yet arrived, and the religious leaders were powerless to trap Jesus until He allowed it.

WEEK FIVE

Questions of the Heart

*"The good man brings good things out of the good stored up in his heart,
and the evil man brings evil things out of the evil stored up in his heart.
For out of the overflow of his heart his mouth speaks."*

LUKE 6:45

As we begin our lesson today, we'll find Jesus in the temple courts after being confronted by the chief priests, teachers of the law, and elders.

Read Mark 12:1–12.

In the culture of the time, it was common for the wealthy to set up vineyards and then lease them to farmers, who would take care of them. At harvest, the landlords would typically send agents to collect a portion of their vineyard's crop as rent for the use of the land. Although the religious leaders didn't fully understand the parable, they did recognize that Jesus was referring to them when He said the land owner would kill the tenants and give the vineyard to others. They were angry, but they were also afraid the crowds would turn on them if they attempted to do anything to Jesus.

In the readings that follow, we will see several attempts on the part of the religious leaders to bait Jesus into saying something that would turn the crowds against Him.

Read Mark 12:13–17.

Jesus was not deceived by the Pharisees' flattery (undue or insincere praise). This tax was unpopular with the Jews because it went directly into the Roman emperor's treasury and represented their defeat by the Romans."[25] This was a clever choice of topics by the Pharisees. Yet, Jesus amazed them with His ability to sidestep the religious leaders' scheme.

Flattery is almost always delivered with impure motives. When someone is flattering you, I caution you to be on your guard. It is a form of manipulation and often stems from resentment and usually is exercised with a hidden agenda.

> Flattery is almost always delivered with impure motives.

One of the most difficult situations I ever faced could have been avoided if I had simply trusted my initial instincts and avoided someone who was dishing out large doses of unearned praise. My spirit told me to be on guard, but I chalked it up to preconceived ideas and ignored the caution signs placed before me. Besides, I have to admit there was a part of me that wanted to believe the flattery.

Have you ever taken the bait of someone's insincere or undue praise? If so, what did you learn from that experience? (Be careful not to dishonor anyone with your answer.)

_____

_____

_____

Now, let's see what other "bait" the religious leaders sent Jesus' way.

Read Mark 12:18–27 and note what the Sadducees did not believe in, according to verse 18:

_____

The Sadducees were posing a question that seemed innocent enough except that they didn't even believe in resurrection. They were not really looking for an answer from Jesus. They were only attempting to make the idea of resurrection appear silly. Jesus' response? He rebuked them for their lack of understanding.

There will not be marriage in heaven. What else do you learn from Revelation 21:1–5?

_____

_____

_____

_____

WEEK FIVE

Sometimes we too make the mistake of putting heaven on the same level with Earth. But our life after the resurrection will bring a whole new level of existence. Everything will be made new!

Please read Mark 12:28–34.

Love your God and love your neighbor as yourself. That sounds so simple, but it is certainly not easy. Most of us can handle, "You shall not steal" (Exodus 20:15) or "You shall not murder" (Exodus 20:13). Many of us feel we have the "love God" part down pretty well. But "love your neighbor as yourself"? That is probably one of the greatest struggles each of us will have this side of heaven. Yet Jesus said it was one of the most important commandments.

Why do you think we struggle so much with loving others?

_____

_____

_____

_____

_____

"And from then on no one dared ask him any more questions" (Mark 12:34). The tables had been turned.

Now read Mark 12:35–40.

I would imagine the teachers of the law were a bit agitated. Not only did Jesus point out an error in their understanding, but He insulted them as well. The key words are "for a show." Jesus revealed to everyone that the acts of the religious leaders were intended to impress others and really had no correlation to their devotion to God. In contrast, our next reading depicts true devotion.

Read Mark 12:41–44.

This widow put nothing impressive into the treasury. Many probably scoffed at her petty offering. Yet Jesus saw a heart overflowing with pure devotion and a grateful spirit.

Read the following passages and note what insight you gain about the importance God places on the motives of our hearts.

1 Samuel 16:7

_____

_____

Proverbs 17:3

_____

_____

Luke 6:45 in the King James Version tells us, "A good man out of the good treasure of his heart bringeth forth that which is good; and an evil man out of the evil treasure of his heart bringeth forth that which is evil: for of the abundance of the heart his mouth speaketh."

The questions posed by the religious leaders "spoketh" much about the inward condition of their hearts. Take a moment to honestly examine your own heart. Of the passages we've studied today, which ones spoke to you the most and why?

_____

_____

_____

_____

_____

_____

In His Time

*At that time men will see the Son of Man coming in clouds
with great power and glory.*

MARK 13:26

Today we come upon what I consider to be some of the most difficult material of our journey together. There are many interpretations of these passages, but the main point we need to glean from this lesson is this: Jesus will, without a doubt, one day return. Everything we study today is intended to reinforce that basic truth as well as help us identify what our focus should be as we wait.

We left off yesterday with Jesus and the disciples at the temple. Let's see what conversation took place as they were leaving.

Please read Mark 13:1–4.

The structure of the temple wasn't like the buildings of today, with brick upon brick held together with mortar or cement. Some of the "massive stones" the disciples described were forty feet long, twelve feet high, and eighteen feet wide.[26] I'm sure it was quite a majestic sight. Jesus' statement that "not one stone" would be left on another was surely hard to comprehend. It doesn't surprise me a bit that Peter was among the disciples who wanted more information. They got a little more than they bargained for!

Read Mark 13:5–13.

Jesus warned the disciples not to be deceived by anyone setting himself up as the Messiah. Jesus alone is Savior and they were to remain faithful to their mission to preach the gospel to all nations. He wanted them to understand that wars, earthquakes, and famines are part of life this side of eternity. He did not want them to become alarmed and lose their focus on what was most important. They would be despised by men, but would have to endure and remain loyal to the message of salvation.

Do you often have difficulty focusing on what is important when you face trials? I know I do. How does this test challenge you?

_____

_____

_____

_____

Read Mark 13:14–23.

The Hebrew expression "abomination that causes desolation" literally means "the profanation that appalls" and comes from a prophecy of Daniel. It first occurred when the Syrian king Antiochus had a pig sacrificed on the altar in Jerusalem, set up brothels in the sacred courts, and placed a statue of Zeus before the Holy Place in the temple, ordering the Jews to worship it.[27] In these passages, Jesus warned the disciples it would happen again.

> The Hebrew expression "abomination that causes desolation" literally means "the profanation that appalls" and comes from a prophecy of Daniel.

Sadly, it did just a few years after Jesus' death. The Jewish historian Josephus recorded appalling profaning of the temple in AD 67–68.[28] The incident preceded the fall of the temple to the Roman army in AD 70. Just as Jesus had told His disciples, the temple was completely destroyed. Hundreds of thousands who sought safety in Jerusalem were killed. Only those who fled "to the mountains," as Jesus instructed, survived.

Now, there is a key quotation of Jesus that Mark did not include in his gospel. It helps us make the transition from the events Jesus foretold would happen at the temple in AD 70 and those that will happen at His second coming.

Read Luke 21:24. According to this passage, who will trample Jerusalem, including the temple?

_____

How long does this verse indicate the Gentiles will trample the temple?

Paul gives more insight into the "times of the Gentiles" in his letter to the Romans.

Please read Romans 11:25–32.

Paul referred to it as the time "until the full number of Gentiles has come in." Let's take a peek ahead and read Peter's words regarding this subject.

Please read 2 Peter 3:3–9.

God doesn't want a single soul to perish. He is patient and waits until the appointed time when His Son will return to Earth and gather His people together to join Him in heaven for all eternity.

The rest of Mark, chapter 13, is dedicated to Jesus' teaching about the events that will take place at His second coming.

Please read Mark 13:24–37.

The Greek word translated "generation" in verse 30 is *genea*. It means "a generation, by implication an age, nation or time." It is derived from the Greek word *genos*, meaning "born, countrymen, diversity, generation, kindred, nation, offspring, stock."

Jesus said the Jewish nation, or race, would not pass away before He returns. The Jewish people have endured horrible persecution throughout history, yet they have survived as a people, just as Jesus said.

He will return at the appointed time "in the clouds with great power and glory!" Jesus knew we human beings would be terribly curious about the time of His return. Our nature is to ask questions and find answers to anything we do not understand. But Jesus was clear no one knows the day or hour, not even Jesus Himself.

According to Mark 13:32, who knows the time of Jesus' return?

What do the following passages indicate we should do while we await Jesus' return?

1 Thessalonians 5:1–11

_____

_____

Jude 17–21

_____

> Jesus will return one day, just as He said.

_____

Jesus will return one day, just as He said. Until that time, we are to build each other up and encourage one another.
We are each a work in progress and we all will fail at times to stay on track. But praise God He will continue working on us until the day Jesus comes again.

What assurance do we have according to Philippians 1:6?

_____

_____

As a way of closing, take a moment to think back through the lessons of the week. What major insight did Peter gain that you think might have helped him in his role as an apostle?

_____

_____

_____

_____

Personal Application

Application for Day One

Jesus entered Jerusalem on the back of a donkey and people placed their cloaks at His feet, acknowledging Him as king. But the people failed to understand that the ride into Jerusalem required a far greater act of surrender on the part of God. As we will see in our upcoming lessons, for Jesus to reign as King, God had to surrender the very life of His one and only Son. Let's reflect on another courageous act of surrender that involved a willful journey upon the back of a donkey.

Please read Genesis 22:1–18.

As he laid his son upon that altar, Abraham must have been in deep agony. Yet Abraham willingly took that journey to surrender his son. He trusted God without question, and "because he did not withhold" something as precious as his son, all nations on earth have been blessed.

> Abraham's ride upon a donkey was a foreshadowing of God's surrender of His one and only Son, Jesus.

Abraham's ride upon a donkey was a foreshadowing of God's surrender of His one and only Son, Jesus. I wonder if Jesus reflected on Abraham's journey to the altar as He took His ride on the donkey into Jerusalem that day.

Read Hebrews 11:17–19 and note what gave Abraham the courage to obey God's strange instructions.

_____

_____

_____

Abraham trusted God so much he believed that if God was calling him to sacrifice his son, He would somehow raise him from the dead. That's exactly what God did with Jesus. Don't you just love the consistency of God's Word?

I asked you on Day One what "cloak" you needed to surrender. Look back at your answer on page 89. Four days later, is it still surrendered or have you picked it up and put it back around your shoulders? If it is still surrendered, rejoice! If not, ask God to give you the courage to lay it upon the altar, trusting Him, as Abraham did, to handle the details.

Application for Day Two

What does Jesus say the temple is to be called, according to Mark 11:17?

_____

Prayer is our connection with our heavenly Father; it is the means by which we communicate and build a relationship with Him. The Pharisees went through the motions in their religious activities, but their hearts were far from God. They seemed to know about God and about the history of His faithful provision, but they didn't look for God's activity in their daily lives.

Read Habakkuk 3:1–2.

Habakkuk knew of God's "fame," and of His acts on behalf of His people. He cried out to God, asking Him to act again. He begged God to dazzle the people with His awesome deed—to do a mighty work among them. God faithfully brought His people out from under the oppression of the Egyptians. He parted the waters of the Jordan River and brought His people into the land of milk and honey. God performed mighty works long ago, and He still performs mighty works today.

> The next time you face a trial, I challenge you to pray as Habakkuk did.

The next time you face a trial, I challenge you to pray as Habakkuk did. I encourage you to locate an example in Scripture of when God moved in a mighty way on behalf of His people. Ask Him to do it again. Ask Him to do a work such as that in your life. He just may part the waters of dissension or strife and provide a clear path for you to find a "land of milk and honey" on the other side. Pray with eager anticipation and watch Him move on your behalf.

Application for Day Three

On Day Three of this week, we discovered that Jesus said two commandments are most important. The first is to love God.

What is the second? (Mark 12:28–34)

_____

The Greek word translated "love" in Mark 12:31 is *agapeo*. This kind of love is deep and unconditional. Closely associated with *agapeo* is the Greek word *agape*. It can be translated "charity" or "benevolence." Agape love places the needs of others above our own, without expectation or condition. It involves loving others as God loves you. It is the kind of love described in 1 Corinthians 13:4–13. Please read those verses now and list some of the characteristics of agape love:

_____

_____

> You are incapable of showing agape love without God.

You are incapable of showing agape love without God. The only way any of us can love others unconditionally, as these verses describe, is by allowing God to pour out His love through us. It is by our *agape* that others will know we are disciples of Christ (John 13:35). Is there someone God is calling you to *agapeo* (love even if you don't feel like it)? What is one way you can *agape* them (show love and affection toward them)?

_____

Do it this week. Don't put it off. The blessing will be yours as well!

Application for Day Four

As we await Jesus' return, we are to encourage and build one another up.

Read Philippians 1:1–6.

How did Paul encourage the saints at Philippi?

_____

While Paul's words are still fresh in your mind, write a note of encouragement to someone who is a partner with you in spreading the gospel. Be specific about the areas where this person serves within the body of Christ. Remind her (or him) that God will continue to work in and through her until the day Christ returns.

That concludes our fifth week of study. You're halfway done! Let me close our lesson today by encouraging you with another wonderful passage:

And let us not be weary in well doing: for in due season we shall reap, if we faint not. As we have therefore opportunity, let us do good unto *all men,* especially unto them who are of the household of faith. Galatians 6:9–10 KJV

WEEK FIVE

Week 6
Revealing Responses

Outpouring Hearts

Then Mary took about a pint of pure nard, an expensive perfume; she poured it on Jesus' feet and wiped his feet with her hair. And the house was filled with the fragrance of the perfume.

JOHN 12:3

Peter had traveled with Jesus for approximately three years at this point in our journey. Nothing could have prepared Peter for the experiences we will study the next two weeks. Keep the tissues close by.

Please begin today by reading Mark 14:1–9.

This alabaster jar was filled with "costly perfume made of pure nard, an aromatic oil from a rare plant root native to India."[29] It was worth as much as a man could make in an entire year at that time.

According to John 12:3, who was this woman? _____

The monetary value of the alabaster jar and its contents was overwhelming. But for a woman, the oil would have had an even greater personal value. There weren't bathtubs or fragrant soaps available at that time. This expensive fragrance would have helped Mary feel clean, beautiful, and feminine.

> The monetary value of the alabaster jar and its contents was overwhelming. But for a woman, the oil would have had an even greater personal value.

The alabaster jar, broken for Jesus, was a precious outpouring of Mary's love and praise for her Lord. She obviously loved Jesus deeply. She lavishly poured the perfume, from His head all the way to His feet. Then she tenderly dried His feet with her hair. Mary withheld nothing for herself. It was an outpouring of love—an act of worship as pure as the contents of that jar.

Read Mark 14:10–11.

Mary's act of love and devotion was starkly contrasted by the betrayal of Judas.

What does John 12:4–6 tell you about Judas Iscariot?

_____

Judas was probably upset about Mary's wasteful anointing because there was no way for him to profit from her offering.

Look back at Mark 14:11. What did the chief priests promise to do for Judas when he led them to Jesus?

_____

I wonder if Mary's outpouring of love fueled this outpouring of greed.

Now read Mark 14:12–17 and Luke 22:7–8.

Who prepared the Passover meal? _____ and _____

Peter and John most likely slaughtered the Passover lamb themselves and roasted it on the fire. They would have prepared unleavened bread (bread without yeast) and bitter herbs. When Jesus and the other ten disciples arrived, Peter and John had everything prepared. What Jesus did next is one of the greatest examples to believers in all Scripture.

Please read John 13:1–17.

I can just imagine the shock on Peter's face as Jesus wrapped that towel around His waist, poured the water into the basin, and began to wash the disciples' dusty, calloused feet. Peter struggled with many things. He spoke at inappropriate times; he often blurted out the wrong thing at the wrong time. But Peter wrestled most with an overwhelming sense of unworthiness.

"No, you shall never wash my feet" were not words of defiance, but words of a man deeply moved by Jesus' outpouring of love.

Look back at Peter's words in Luke 5:7–8.

Peter loved Jesus with pure devotion. He was overwhelmed at the thought of the same Jesus who had been transfigured before Him placing Himself in the position of a common servant by washing the feet of this "sinful man."

If Peter didn't allow Jesus to wash his feet, what did Jesus say would happen, according to John 13:8?

_____

_____

The Greek word translated "part" is *meros*. It means "to get a section or allotment, a division or share." Jesus was telling Peter he could not share a relationship with Jesus if he refused to allow Jesus to cleanse him.

What was Peter's response? _____

Based on the personalities of the twelve disciples, what do you think the reaction of some of the other men might have been? Have fun with this question. Consider a number of possibilities and be prepared to share your speculations with your small group.

_____

_____

_____

_____

On a more serious note, have you allowed Jesus to fully cleanse you? What do you think your reaction would

> Have you allowed Jesus to fully cleanse you?

have been had you been in that upper room? Do you, like Peter, harbor such feelings of unworthiness that you are resistant to Jesus' cleansing love? You may know you have been cleansed and forgiven, but have you fully embraced it with your heart? Take a moment to think about these questions. Please write down your thoughts:

_____

_____

_____

Accept His love today. Allow Him to pour out His love upon you and wash your feet. This time, truly accept it. Then go and wash the feet of others. Help them experience the Savior's love through your loving acts of humble service. May that service truly come from the outpouring of a grateful heart.

WEEK SIX   DAY TWO

The Cup of Redemption

"This is my blood of the covenant, which is poured out for many,"
he said to them.

Mark 14:24

Jesus was symbolically anointed by Mary and prepared for burial by her emotional anointing with perfume from her alabaster jar. Peter and John were selected to prepare the Passover meal, and once it was prepared, Jesus washed the feet of His disciples in a tender outpouring of His own. Truly there is no greater indication of the love God has for each of us than the cleansing we have received and continue to receive through our Lord and Savior Jesus.

Today we will focus on the Passover Meal that took place in the Upper Room. It was the final meal Jesus had with His disciples before He was crucified, and it was rich in symbolism.

Read Mark 14:12–21.

In Jesus' day, during Passover, the lambs were taken to the temple and personally slain by the persons offering them.[30] So Peter and John would have taken the lamb to the temple to slaughter it. The blood would have been poured out on the altar and the fat burned. Then Peter and John would have returned to the upper room to roast it and prepare the unleavened bread and bitter herbs.

> In Jesus' day, during Passover, the lambs were taken to the temple and personally slain by the persons offering them.

The lamb was sacrificed in remembrance of the lambs slain at the first Passover, when God saved the Israelites from destruction and brought them safely out of bondage in Egypt. The unleavened bread was called the "Bread of Affliction." It represented the Israelites' (then called "Hebrews") slavery to the Egyptians before they were rushed out of Egypt so quickly they couldn't add yeast to their bread. The bitter herbs symbolized the bitter tears of the Hebrews when they were slaves to the Egyptians as well as the tears shed by the Egyptians over the deaths of their firstborn sons.

Along with food, wine was served at the Passover, and it too had significance. God made four promises to Moses when He said He would bring the people of Israel out of Egypt. Four cups of wine were served at the Passover meal, each representing one of those promises.

Read Exodus 6:6–7 and see the chart on p. 112 (from three sources: *Feasts of the Lord* [Howard & Rosenthaul] *Last Supper, Lord's Supper* [Howard Marshall] and *Keeping Passover* [Ira Steinroot]):

> The Passover has changed a little since the time of Jesus. But it is still regimented and always follows the same basic pattern.

The Passover has changed a little since the time of Jesus. But it is still regimented and always follows the same basic pattern. The meal begins with the pouring of the first cup of wine (The Cup of Sanctification) and the reciting of a blessing. Next, the leader (in this case, Jesus) takes a bowl of water around to each guest, allowing the guests to wash their hands. The hand washing is a symbolic act of purification

WEEK SIX

111

CUP AS IDENTIFIED AT PASSOVER MEAL	GOD'S PROMISE AS OUTLINED IN EXODUS 6:6–7
1. Cup of Sanctification	I will bring you out from under the yoke of the Egyptians (v.6).
2. Cup of Proclamation	I will free you from being slaves to them (v. 6).
3. Cup of Redemption	I will redeem you with an outstretched arm and with mighty acts of judgment (v.6).
4. Cup of Acceptance and Praise	I will take you as my own people and I will be your God (v.7).

as the participants prepare to handle the food. It was probably at this point in the meal Jesus washed the disciples' feet. The first food that is served is green herbs, dipped in salt water, which reminds guests of the tears of pain and suffering the Hebrews experienced while enslaved in Egypt.

After serving the green herbs, Jesus would have broken one of three loaves of unleavened bread, which is called the "Bread of Affliction." It is tradition for the youngest person attending the meal to ask a set of questions about the original Passover and the Exodus. After the questions have been asked, the second cup of wine, the Cup of Proclamation, is served. It is at this point in the meal the Passover story is told. Then the lamb is served.[31]

Now read Mark 14:22–26.

The cup served with the meal is the third cup. Look at the chart above. What is the third cup called?

Jesus chose to implement what we call Communion at the serving of the third cup. For the Jews, the Passover has always been "closely associated with the fervent hope for the coming Messiah."[32] It is after the third cup the youngest guest at the meal opens the front door in hopes Elijah (prophesied to precede the Messiah) will come in and announce the Messiah's arrival. As we discussed earlier in our study, John the Baptist came in the spirit and power of Elijah and fulfilled this prophecy.

Jesus' shed blood and His broken body brought ultimate redemption for all people. Jesus was not asking the disciples to literally drink His blood, but to drink of the cup that represents the redemption of God's people through the shedding of His blood.

At the closing of the Passover meal, a final cup of wine is poured and then Psalms 113–118 are sung. Write out Psalm 118:21–22 in your own words:

_____

_____

_____

_____

Although I'm sure he didn't understand at the time, Peter later determined the significance of the words he sang with Jesus at the Last Supper. Who does Peter indicate is the "stone the builders rejected and the capstone" in Acts 4:8–12?

_____

The entire Passover meal was instituted by God to commemorate the freeing of God's people from bondage through the shedding of the blood of the lamb.

According to 1 Corinthians 5:6–8, who is our Passover Lamb? _____

Just as the Israelites had been set free from bondage by the blood of the lamb covering their doorposts, believers in Christ have been set free from the condemnation of the law of sin and death by His blood poured out for us on the cross.

Every time we partake of Holy Communion, we remember the body of Jesus broken and His blood shed. We drink from the Cup of Redemption that reconciled us to our heavenly Father.

Read Matthew 26:29.

One day we will drink from the fourth cup (the Cup of Acceptance and Praise) with Jesus in His Father's kingdom! I wonder if we'll sing the words of this closing hymn:

> *You are my God, and I will give you thanks; you are my God,*
> *and I will exalt you.*
> *Give thanks to the LORD, for he is good; his love endures forever.*
>
> PSALM 118:28–29

WEEK SIX

The Flesh Is Weak

The spirit truly is ready, but the flesh is weak.

Mark 14:38 KJV

Yesterday, we examined the final meal Jesus had with His disciples and explored the symbolism contained in the ceremony. Just after the Passover Meal, Jesus made some disturbing predictions.

Please read Mark 14:27–31 and write Peter's words as recorded in verse 29:

_____

_____

The word "I" in this verse is emphatic and indicates that Peter was claiming greater allegiance to Jesus than that of all the other disciples.[33] Just like many of us, Peter desperately wanted to be strong and fully devoted to Jesus. Yet, as we will soon see, his spirit was willing, but his flesh was overwhelmingly weak.

Read Luke 22:31–34.

Satan had asked to sift Peter like wheat. Grain is purified by sifting. In Jesus' day, the grain was placed into large sieves that were shaken vigorously, allowing the grain to pass through. Undesirable pieces or weeds were left behind.[34] Although the idea of being shaken was probably

> Trials of any kind can bring about a level of spiritual sifting.

Peter's focus, it was likely encouraging to know he would be purified in the process.

I believe a sifting by Satan occurs when everything in our lives is shaken to the point where we have nothing to cling to except our faith, but trials of any kind can bring about a level of spiritual sifting. We come through those circumstances stronger and some weeds, such as discontentment or pride, have often been sifted away.

Now read Mark 14:32–42.

What does Jesus ask God to take from Him in verse 36?_____

Based on what you learned in yesterday's lesson, what cup do you think Jesus was talking about?

_____

_____

_____

Everything is possible with God. Jesus knew that God could choose to redeem His people another way. God could have pardoned the sins of His people through some other manner, yet He did not.

For more insight into Jesus' emotions during His prayer in the Garden of Gethsemane, read Luke 22:39–46.

The Greek word translated "anguish" in this passage is *agonia*. It is derived from *agon*, which implies "a contest, an effort or anxiety, conflict, contention, fight, or race." Jesus' flesh and spirit were in conflict as He prayed in that garden. Jesus was fully human and fully God. The human part of Jesus wanted desperately to escape the brutal and agonizing death He was about to endure. Jesus also knew that to take on the sin of all humanity would require He be separated spiritually from His heavenly Father, an anguish even worse than the physical pain.

> The human part of Jesus wanted desperately to escape the brutal and agonizing death He was about to endure.

Jesus knelt there in the garden and prayed in such agony that He was sweating blood, a condition called *hematidrosis*. It is an extremely rare disorder characterized by excretion of blood or blood pigment in the sweat.[35] It is associated with intense psychological stress.

Why did Jesus tell Peter to "watch and pray," according to Mark 14:38?

_____

Jesus was not just informing Peter of his weakness. Jesus Himself was being tempted to flee the cross. His spirit was willing, but His flesh was weak. Jesus gained the strength He

WEEK SIX

needed to overcome His flesh through prayer. If Jesus needed to pray to overcome temptation, don't you think we should do the same?

What is typically your first response when you are being tempted?

_____

_____

How does Jesus' need for prayer encourage or challenge you personally?

_____

_____

_____

_____

_____

> In contrast, Peter slept and rested while Jesus prayed.

_____

Look again at Mark 14:37–38.

Jesus prayed for at least an hour. His sorrow overwhelmed Him to the point of death. Yet He was able to pray, "Not what I will, but what You will." He got up from that prayer time strong and in total submission to God's will.

In contrast, Peter slept and rested while Jesus prayed. He had emphatically proclaimed he would not fall away. He wasn't prepared for the sifting about to take place in his life. Jesus had warned him, yet as we've seen often, Peter wasn't listening. His spirit truly was willing, but his flesh was tragically weak.

Memorable Denial

The Lord turned and looked straight at Peter. Then Peter remembered the word the Lord had spoken to him: "Before the rooster crows today, you will disown me three times."

LUKE 22:61

*J*esus prayed earnestly in the Garden of Gethsemane. Sadly, Peter did not follow Jesus' advice to pray in order to avoid temptation. As a result, he was unable to remain committed to Jesus as he had so boldly proclaimed he would.

As we begin our reading today, we find Jesus and the Twelve still in the garden. The chief priests, teachers of the law, and elders are still on their quest to trap Jesus. As we will see, this time Jesus allows them to succeed.

Read Mark 14:43–47.

What signal had Judas arranged with the crowd?_____

To betray Jesus with a kiss was the ultimate betrayal. Judas called Jesus, "Rabbi," which was an official Hebrew title of honor. I would imagine the other disciples were appalled by the scene unfolding before them.

According to John 18:10–11, who cut off the ear of the high priest's servant?

_____

Jesus told Peter to put his sword away and again made reference to the Cup of Redemption, "the blood of the covenant," which would be poured out for many as He hung on the cross.

Peter acted with impulsive determination. However, as the evening continued, that determination turned to trepidation and eventually denial.

Read Mark 14:48–54.

According to verse 54, where did Peter follow Jesus?

_____

The other disciples had "deserted him and fled," but Peter followed Jesus at a distance. Peter was deeply committed to Jesus. He desired to be faithful to his Master. He desperately wanted to keep his word and die with Jesus if necessary. But his flesh was weak. He had distanced himself from Christ and was communing with the Enemy.

Read Mark 14:55–72 and Luke 22:60–62.

Peter evidently was able to see Jesus throughout the entire interrogation. And Jesus could hear Peter's words of denial.

According to Luke 22:61, what did Jesus do just after the rooster crowed?

_____

Peter had denied Jesus three times. As he looked into the eyes of his Lord, Master, and Friend, the full impact of what had taken place crashed down upon him. Peter "wept bitterly."

It occurs to me that Peter's denial began before the servant girl ever said a word to him. Had he spoken up when Jesus was falsely accused? When people fabricated stories, did Peter correct them? When the character of Jesus was questioned, did Peter come to His defense? Peter had already begun to deny Christ with his silence.

> It occurs to me that Peter's denial began before the servant girl ever said a word to him.

My background is in accounting and personnel management. One day I was having a discussion with my boss about the actions of a rather defiant employee. After listening to the facts regarding the rebellious worker, the business-minded owner of the company said, "It is time for us to have a "come-to-Jesus meeting." I was stunned. I had never heard that expression. I sat there silent for a moment with my mind racing as I struggled to absorb the full meaning of her comment. I knew the businesswoman was not a Christian. Her tone and words portrayed Jesus as a heavy-handed, merciless judge.

My first instinct was to ask her what she meant. My spirit cried out, "You don't know Him!" Yet, I sat there in stunned silence. I had known Jesus for years. I'd experienced His grace, His mercy, and His unfailing love. I knew I had an opportunity to share the mercy and grace of Jesus with this accomplished, respected woman. I had spoken to Jesus just that morning through prayer. I loved Him. Yet I didn't say a word. I didn't ask her if she knew my Savior. I just simply said nothing. In essence, I denied Jesus with my silence.

We can deny knowing Jesus in many ways—with silence, with our lifestyle choices, with our attitudes, or with words. Has there ever been a time when you denied Jesus in one of these ways? If so, briefly describe the circumstances:

_____

_____

_____

_____

I encourage you to write a prayer of confession and commit to responding differently in the future:

_____

_____

_____

_____

_____

Please look up Romans 8:1 and write it here in your own words:

_____

_____

Though we all fail from time to time, I praise God that because of our faith in Jesus, we are not condemned.

We have learned much from our journey with Peter this week. We've seen an outpouring of love from Mary (sister of Martha and Lazarus) and from Jesus. We've attended the Passover Meal and recognized Jesus as the true Passover Lamb. We've learned that although our spirits are often willing, without prayer, we are defeated by the weaknesses of our flesh. And we've witnessed Peter's painful denial of his relationship with our Lord.

We're not quite done. Tomorrow, we will briefly review these lessons and draw some additional insights to apply to our lives.

WEEK SIX　DAY FIVE

Personal Application

Application for Day One

Mary anointed Jesus with the costly oil in her alabaster jar. Let's take a look at a similar outpouring from another grateful heart.

Please read Luke 7:36–48.

"Your sins are forgiven." Those are some of the most precious words that ever formed on our Savior's lips. Perhaps, like me, you've been forgiven much. No costly perfume or generous gift in the offering plate could ever compare to the forgiveness we've found and the love we've received from our Savior Jesus. Yet we sometimes struggle to simply give a small portion of our belongings and time to our Lord. The sinful woman gave it all—a lavish outpouring from her grateful heart.

Pretend for a moment you have a beautiful and expensive alabaster jar of perfume worth a year's wages. If you were to pour it out as an offering upon Jesus, what would it represent to you? Would it symbolize the forgiveness you've received for years of sin and costly mistakes? Or freedom from the guilt you felt every time you failed to meet human expectations? Perhaps, like this woman, there have been people in your life who have made you feel like an unworthy, sinful woman, yet you've found love and acceptance at the feet of Jesus.

_____

_____

_____

The next time you attend church, consider your answer and ask God to give you the courage to give extravagantly, as this sinful woman did.

Application for Day Two

At the Passover Meal in the Upper Room with His disciples, Jesus instituted what we call "Communion," or "The Lord's Supper."

Read 1 Corinthians 11:23–26.

According to verse 26, what are we proclaiming when we eat the bread and drink the cup?

_____

Continue by reading 1 Corinthians 11:27–28 and note the warning contained in these verses:

_____

_____

_____

When we partake of Communion, we are to do so with reverence and awe. We should think about the sacrifice Jesus was willing to make on our behalf. The next time you partake of the bread and the cup, take a moment to first examine your motives and search your heart. In next week's lessons, we will study Christ's death on the cross. I pray those lessons enable you to discover a fresh sense of holy "awe."

Application for Day Three

On Day Three, we learned that Jesus prayed to overcome the conflict between His human nature (flesh) and His Spirit. Jesus warned Peter to do the same in order to avoid falling into temptation. Jesus prayed for at least an hour that night, then arose strong and ready to face the cross. In contrast, Peter slept. I would imagine the hours that followed were replayed in Peter's mind for the rest of his life.

> If Jesus had to pray to His Father to overcome His human nature, why do we think we can overcome ours on our own?

If Jesus had to pray to His Father to overcome His human nature, why do we think we can overcome ours on our own? I relate to Peter. There have been times I underestimated the power of my carnal nature and forged forward totally unprepared to deal with life's temptations.

How are you doing with the discipline of prayer? Our flesh is weak. Regardless of the depth of our desire to live committed to Christ, if we aren't consistent with prayer, we will lack the power needed to overcome our sinful natures. On the graph below, indicate the frequency of your focused, uninterrupted prayer time.

| Never | Rarely | During Trials | Sometimes | Weekly | Daily |

Take Jesus' words personally: "Watch and pray so that you will not fall into temptation. The spirit is willing, but the body is weak" (Mark 14:38).

Application for Day Four

On Day Four we witnessed Peter's humiliating denial of Jesus.

Read Mark 14:53–54.

According to verse 54, what did Peter do in the courtyard of the high priest?

Peter's actions just before his denial of Christ contain valuable lessons for us today. His first mistake was a lack of prayer. His second mistake was distancing himself from Jesus. His third? Based on the passages you just read, take a guess.

> Peter's actions just before his denial of Christ contain valuable lessons for us today.

_____

You got it—lingering in opposing territory. Peter distanced himself from his Lord and then plopped right down and warmed himself at the fire.

Who asked to sift Peter like wheat according to Luke 22:31? _____

Satan is the true enemy of every believer. Without a doubt, this warm fire in the courtyard was strategically planned with Peter in mind. Distanced from the Lord, Peter rested awhile and found warmth in opposing territory.

Can you think of some ways that we, in today's society, seek warmth in opposing territory?

_____

_____

_____

When we distance ourselves from the Lord, we begin to find comfort in the things of the world. Like Peter, when we linger too long in a worldly situation, our resolve to remain faithful can become distant. If you've distanced yourself from Jesus lately, you are in dangerous territory. Seek reconnection with God and find your rest in Him alone.

WEEK SIX

Week 7

Defeat Gives Way to Victory

Crowned with Thorns

*They put a purple robe on him, then twisted together a crown
of thorns and set it on him.*

MARK 15:17

*L*ast week we witnessed Peter's internal struggles as he followed Jesus through the last day of His earthly ministry. Our last glimpse of Peter was of a man broken and humiliated by his weakness and betrayal. Scripture doesn't tell us where Peter went or what he did while Jesus was sentenced and crucified, but today we will study the events that took place as Jesus was brought before Pilate.

Begin by reading Mark 15:1.

Before reading further, let's take a look at the decision made by the chief priests, elders, and teachers of the law.

Read Luke 22:66–23:2.

By suggesting that Jesus opposed taxes to Caesar, the religious leaders were accusing Him of an act of treason against the Roman government—a crime punishable by death. His claim to be the Messiah was also understood to be a statement of defiance against the Roman government and considered blasphemy by the Jews. The religious leaders obviously had their minds set on having Jesus executed.

Now read Mark 15:1–5.

According to verse 5, what was Jesus' response to the numerous accusations against Him?

> By suggesting that Jesus opposed taxes to Caesar, the religious leaders were accusing Him of an act of treason against the Roman government—a crime punishable by death.

_____

_____

Hold your place in Mark, and look up Isaiah 53:7 and write it here in your own words:

_____

_____

_____

_____

The prophet Isaiah foretold Jesus' death seven centuries before it happened. As Jesus was accused, He did not open His mouth, but allowed Himself to be led as the Lamb of God to the slaughter.

Please read Mark 15:6–12.

Pilate evidently assumed (and hoped), when he asked what the crowds wanted him to do with Jesus, the people would request that Jesus be released. But the chief priests had been working far too hard, for far too long, to allow that to happen. They "stirred up" that crowd to influence Pilate to release Barabbas instead.

What happened next gives me goosebumps every time I read it. Picture yourself standing among the crowd. Visualize Jesus standing accused (falsely, no less), on a platform before you.

Now read Mark 15:13–15.

What did the crowd shout? _____

Pilate had Jesus flogged. He was "stripped, probably tied to a post, and beaten on the back by several guards using short leather whips studded with sharp pieces of bone or metal. Often this punishment was fatal."[36] The vicious flogging was only the beginning of the brutality and humiliation Jesus endured that day. Let's see what happened next.

Read Mark 15:16–20.

The soldiers took Jesus to the Praetorium, which was the judgment hall of the Roman governor.[37]

What did the soldiers place upon Jesus' head?

_____

The crown had an astounding, unintended, spiritual significance.

Please read Genesis 2:15–17.

What tree was forbidden? _____

Adam and Eve were originally allowed to eat from the Tree of Life, along with every other tree in Eden, with the exception of the tree of the knowledge of good and evil. They also had the opportunity to live forever with God in the garden. But once they ate of the forbidden tree, life changed.

Now read Genesis 3:17–24.

According to verse 22, why were Adam and Eve banished from the garden?

_____

The sin of Adam and Eve caused all humanity to fall under a curse. Once they sinned, God could no longer allow the couple to eat from the Tree of Life. Had they eaten of the Tree of Life, they would have then lived forever in a sinful state and the entire human race would have remained forever separated from God.

> Adam and Eve were banished from the garden for their own protection.

As part of the curse, what did God say the ground would produce?

WEEK SEVEN

Adam and Eve were banished from the garden for their own protection. That crown of thorns placed mockingly upon Jesus' head was a profound representation of the curse placed upon humanity. It overwhelms me to think of the sacrifice Jesus willingly made for us.

Those thorns that pierced our Savior's brow represented your sin and my sin. Regardless of what sins we've committed or how far we've fallen, Jesus willingly allowed the soldiers to mock Him and spit upon Him so He could bring you (and me) back into fellowship with our heavenly Father.

WEEK SEVEN | DAY TWO

Near the Cross

Near the cross of Jesus stood his mother, his mother's sister,
Mary the wife of Clopas, and Mary Magdalene.

JOHN 19:25

*J*esus was tried, convicted, and flogged. He was then handed over to be crucified. Today we will stand near the cross with a loyal group of women as they witness Jesus' crucifixion. We will discover the significance of the words Jesus spoke while on the cross. We will seek to understand some of the emotions Jesus might have struggled with as He prepared to be separated from His Father.

Begin today's Bible reading with Mark 15:21–39.

What did Jesus cry out in a loud voice, according to verse 34?

"In Judaism, when a Bible verse is cited its entire context is implied, if appropriate".[38] The words of Jesus were the first words of Psalm 22. This psalm describes, in amazing detail, much of what happened on the cross that day.

Read Psalm 22:1–8.

Note every reference you can find in this passage to Jesus' sentencing and death on the cross:

_____

_____

_____

_____

_____

Everything that happened to Jesus that day was for a purpose. He is the Messiah and Savior of the world. What you have noted is only a portion of all that was foretold about the events of Jesus' death. The religious leaders should have recognized Him. They should have believed.

Be prepared to discuss your answers with your small group at your next meeting. Each person may have slightly different answers and everyone will gain from the knowledge shared in your group. If you know of other prophecies fulfilled during the Crucifixion, I encourage you to note them here:

_____

_____

_____

_____

Take time to consider the impossibility of all these prophecies being fulfilled through one man, apart from God's design.

According to John 19:28–30, what were Jesus' words just before He died?

_____

Now read Matthew 27:50–52.

What happened when Jesus "gave up His spirit"?

_____

After witnessing all this, what conclusion did the centurion come to, according to Mark 15:39?

_____

_____

Jesus is the Son of God and He willingly laid down His life for you and for me. When His work on the cross was finished, all Creation shook as the Creator Himself gave up His Spirit.

Read Mark 15:40–41.

The women who served and followed Jesus were important to Jesus' ministry. According to Luke 8:1–3, what did the women do for Jesus' ministry?

_____

The women supported Jesus' ministry by "their own means." More than likely, they wove fabrics and sold them at the market (Proverbs 31:17–24). Sometimes women feel they have no relevant place in the body of Christ. But the women in Jesus' life should be an encouragement to all of us.

> Eleven of the twelve apostles had failed Jesus either through betrayal, denial, or abandonment.

Where were the women positioned, according to John 19:25?

_____

Eleven of the twelve apostles had failed Jesus either through betrayal, denial, or abandonment. Only John (referred to as "the disciple whom [Jesus] loved") stood with the loyal group of women (John 19:26).

The women stood on the hill watching as Jesus was crucified. Crucifixion was a slow and agonizing death by asphyxiation. The shoulders and arms were stretched and pulled out of joint. The nerves in the hands and feet were crushed by large nails. Jesus died in severe physical pain. In addition, He was mocked, insulted, and spit upon. He bore the sin of the world and He experienced the wrath of God as judgment for that sin.

In times of severe physical or emotional pain, most people feel a deep need to be in the presence of God. We seek comfort and strength from our heavenly Father.

What does 2 Corinthians 5:21 tell us Jesus became? _____

Because of the sin Jesus bore on our behalf, He experienced His Father's wrath while hanging on the cross rather than His Father's comfort. I hold back tears as I think of the agony Jesus endured as He died. I can't imagine how the women felt as they stood watching Him. They saw the soldiers mock Him and spit on Him. They watched Him breathe His last breath. Yet these women stood beside Him. They were Jesus' disciples. They followed Him, believed in Him, and took care of Him. They supported His ministry—even at the cross.

How do the actions of this loyal group of women challenge you to a deeper commitment to Jesus Christ?

_____

_____

_____

_____

> As we serve and support the ministry of Jesus Christ by our own means, may we find comfort in knowing that our efforts and our gifts are acceptable to Jesus.

He is the Son of God. He died, just as the Scriptures foretold He would. And He did it willingly for you and for me. Like the women who stood near the cross, may we also be loyal and faithful disciples.

As we serve and support the ministry of Jesus Christ by our own means, may we find comfort in knowing that our efforts and our gifts are acceptable to Jesus. God originally created woman to be a helper to man. I wonder if He thought forward to the day when some committed and loyal women would be helpers for His Son and remain lovingly near Him on the cross as He suffered.

Eyewitness to Majesty

We did not follow cleverly invented stories when we told you about the power and coming of our Lord Jesus Christ, but we were eyewitnesses of his majesty.

2 PETER 1:16

Yesterday we found that the women stood near the cross and remained faithful to Jesus, even at His death. Today we will discover an empty tomb and find that Jesus chose to appear first to two very needy followers.

Please begin today by reading Mark 15:42–47.

As a prominent member of the Sanhedrin, Joseph would have witnessed Jesus' trial in front of that body. How is Joseph described in Luke 23:50–51?

_____

_____

Joseph had not voted for Jesus' conviction. And then He went boldly before Pilate and asked for Jesus' body. He prepared Jesus' body for burial and wrapped it in linen.

In whose tomb was Jesus placed, according to Matthew 27:59–60?

_____

Now read Matthew 27:61–66.

The Marys remained near Jesus even after His death. The tomb was guarded and sealed. The guards made the tomb as secure as they knew how.

Please read Mark 16:1–7.

132

The Marys went to anoint Jesus' body early on Sunday morning. According to verse 6, why was Jesus not in the tomb?

_____

Who were the women to tell (v. 7)? _____

The angel made a point to tell the women to notify Peter. The same Peter who had denied Jesus three times. Yes, Peter, who had disappeared when Jesus died. Yet Peter, along with the other disciples, would see Jesus in Galilee.

Read John 20:1–9.

Now, doesn't that seem like Peter? John ("the disciple whom Jesus loved," according to John 21:20) beat Peter to the scene, yet it was Peter who first stepped into that tomb.

What insight into Peter's thoughts do you gain from John 20:9?

_____

Peter didn't understand that Jesus had risen. He was probably intent on finding evidence of who had taken the body. I imagine he was bewildered by the linen neatly folded and set aside. He was probably indignant anyone would take the body of his beloved friend. Finally, John stepped inside, looked around, and understood.

According to Matthew 28:2–4, how was the stone rolled away from the entrance to the tomb?

_____

_____

The stone was not rolled back by thieves intending to steal the body. It was rolled back by an angel revealing the empty tomb. Jesus had risen!

Look again at Mark 14:28. What were Jesus' words to His disciples just days before?

_____

_____

Peter had pledged a deeper loyalty to Jesus than all the other disciples ("Even if all fall away, I will not" (Mark 14:29)). Yet, as he stood inside the empty tomb, Peter didn't remember Jesus' words to him and the other disciples.

> Peter had pledged a deeper loyalty to Jesus than all the other disciples.

Read John 20:10–18.

Mary was rewarded greatly for her loyalty. She was the first to see the risen Christ! But who does 1 Corinthians 15:3–5 indicate Jesus appeared to next?

John stood by the cross and remained faithful to the very end. Yet Peter is the apostle to whom Jesus chose to appear first. Why? I wonder if Jesus appeared first to those who were most in need of a fresh dose of His presence.

Mary wept at the tomb, wanting to know where His body had been taken. My guess is Peter also wept at the missing body of his beloved Jesus. John had understood, but Peter had not. John had remained faithful, Peter had not. Peter had wanted desperately to be Jesus' most faithful follower. He loved Jesus with all his heart. But I would guess Peter was just as broken and confused as Mary after visiting the empty tomb.

> Peter was an eyewitness to the majesty of Jesus Christ both before and after the cross.

Peter was an eyewitness to the majesty of Jesus Christ both before and after the cross. He walked with Him throughout His entire ministry. He witnessed Jesus' transfiguration. He witnessed His trial. And Peter witnessed the resurrected Christ before any of the other apostles. Peter had a personal and intimate relationship with Jesus. To use Peter's own words:

> *We did not follow cleverly invented stories when we told you about the power and coming of our Lord Jesus Christ, but we were eyewitnesses of his majesty.*
>
> 2 PETER 1:16

Tomorrow we will see Peter once again singled out, this time in front of the others.

Restoring Rebuke

When they had finished eating, Jesus said to Simon Peter,
"Simon son of John, do you truly love me more than these?"

JOHN 21:15

Before His death, Jesus told the apostles that after He had risen He would go ahead of them into Galilee. Let's see what happened.

Please read John 21:1–3.

The Sea of Galilee is also called the Sea of Tiberias. What did Peter say he was going to do there?

_____

I find it interesting that Peter returned to fishing after Jesus' death. Peter left his nets behind to follow Jesus at the beginning of our study. What do you think prompted him to pick them up again?

> I find it interesting that Peter returned to fishing after Jesus' death.

_____

Scripture doesn't tell us why, but having failed a few times in my own Christian walk, I can take a guess. Peter had failed Jesus. He had been prepared over the previous three years for his role as an apostle. He was renamed "The Rock" by Jesus Himself. The angel had specifically mentioned Peter's name when he told Mary to tell the disciples what happened at the tomb. And the resurrected Jesus had appeared to Peter individually (a privilege shared by no other apostle). Yet, it appears Peter was unable to forgive himself for what he had done. Feeling unworthy to carry the title of "The Rock" or "Apostle," Peter tried to return to being Simon the fisherman in Galilee.

When we feel unworthy to commune with the body of Christ, undeserving to serve Him and reflect His glory to the world around us, we often try to slip back into the life we had before we knew Him. We call old friends, visit old hangouts, or turn the radio dial back to the "old station." We quietly drop out of Bible study. We become "too busy" to have our names on the work schedule for Sunday school. We begin to seek comfort under our covers on Sunday mornings rather than seeking the Comforter in the sanctuary.

Can you recall a time when you tried to slip back into old patterns? If so, what caused your backsliding?

_____

_____

If your answer was "Yes," how successful were you at squeezing back into the old mold? Describe how you felt:

_____

_____

_____

According to John 21:3, how successful was Peter?

_____

Peter may have had a few flashbacks. He'd been in this position before.

Re-read Luke 5:4–8 and then read John 21:4–14.

Peter received an abundant catch at the direction of the Lord. I would imagine Peter's shame at denying Jesus was at the forefront of his mind as he brought his net ashore. And breakfast? Well, it probably didn't help.

What kind of fire were the fish cooking on, according to John 21:9?

_____

The Greek word translated "fire of burning coals" here is *anthrakia*. It is used only one other time in the New Testament. Let's look at it and see what memories these coals would have ignited for our friend Peter.

Read John 18:17–18.

The Greek word for "fire" here is the same as for "fire of burning coals" in John 21:9. What was taking place the last time Peter had felt the warmth of a fire of burning coals?

_____

_____

I don't know about you, but I think I would have lost my appetite. Peter stuck around for breakfast, but probably felt about as lively as the cooking fish. Yet Jesus didn't let Peter off the hook easily. (Sorry, I couldn't resist just one more pun!)

Read John 21:15.

How did Jesus address Peter? _____

Whom do you think Jesus was talking about when He said "more than these"?

_____

Re-read Mark 14:29, and note Peter's words, just before he denied the Lord three times.

_____

_____

Peter had declared a deeper loyalty and love for Jesus than all the other disciples. He had said in essence, "I love you more than these guys do. I am devoted to you more than they are." Yet only John stood near the cross. There is no mention of Peter even standing at a distance.

I hope Peter ate light that morning because he had to eat his words after breakfast. Jesus asked Peter, "Do you truly *agapao* me more than these?" Do you remember the definition of *agapao* from our lesson in Week Five? It is a deep, unconditional love that has nothing to do with circumstances.

Peter's response was interesting. He used a different word when he responded to Jesus. It is the Greek word *phileo,* which means "to have affection for, to be fond of, as a friend. It denotes personal attachment as a matter of sentiment or feeling."

In other words, when Jesus asked if Peter loved Him with a pure, unconditional love, regardless of the circumstances, Peter basically responded, "You know I have affection for you." Not the same. Why do you think Peter said this?

_____

_____

_____

Before we analyze this further, let's look at the rest of the conversation. Please read John 21:16–17.

> I believe Peter loved Jesus with pure devotion, far more than simply as a friend or companion. But his actions had reflected less than the love Jesus deserved.

The final time Jesus asked Peter if he loved Him, Jesus changed His word to *phileo.* I picture Peter having difficulty looking Jesus in the eye as they spoke there by the lake. I believe Peter loved Jesus with pure devotion, far more than simply as a friend or companion. But his actions had reflected less than the love Jesus deserved. His actions had not shown *agapeo.* Peter had been humbled. This exchange between Jesus and Peter was certainly a rebuke. But within the wrapping of rebuke was a loving gift of grace and restoration. When Jesus used the word *phileo* in His final question, He basically said, "Peter, I know you can't love me with a totally unselfish love, but even with all your imperfections, I still want you to feed my sheep."

The disciples had probably chastised Peter for his failure numerous times. Jesus rebuked him, yes, but He did it in love and allowed Peter to once again feel accepted. Jesus gave Peter the honored duty of being a shepherd to the flock.

Read John 21:18–19.

What were Jesus' final words to Peter in verse 19? _____

As unworthy as the disciples probably felt Peter was, Jesus lovingly issued a restoring rebuke to Peter in front of all of his peers by the lake that day.

Personal Application

Application for Day One

Jesus went before Pilate and was falsely accused of many things. He acknowledged being the King of the Jews, but other than that, He made no reply. He was led like a lamb to the slaughter. The soldiers put a crown of thorns on His head. He was mocked, beaten, and flogged by the soldiers. Their intent was to humiliate and make fun of this man who claimed to be the Messiah.

Each thorn that pierced His flesh must have reminded Jesus of His mission. Thorns and thistles were part of the curse God placed upon the earth because of sin. Thorns pierced our Lord's earthly flesh that day, but sin must have pierced His divine heart far more.

Read Genesis 6:5–6.

Have you ever considered how your sins have pierced the heart of God? Has it ever occurred to you His heavenly heart can be filled with pain? Write a prayer of confession, but don't just ask God to forgive your sin—tell Him you're sorry for the pain you've caused Him by your actions.

> Each thorn that pierced His flesh must have reminded Jesus of His mission. Thorns and thistles were part of the curse God placed upon the earth because of sin.

_____

_____

_____

_____

Now read 1 John 1:9 and rejoice!

Application for Day Two

Peter wasn't among those near the cross. He had abandoned Jesus even though he desperately wanted to remain faithful. We don't know if he watched from a distance as he had in the courtyard. What we do know is that Peter abandoned his beloved Jesus. However, Jesus didn't abandon Peter. He restored him. Jesus will never abandon us, either.

What do you learn by reading Hebrews 13:5 and 2 Corinthians 4:8–9?

> Peter wasn't among those near the cross. He had abandoned Jesus even though he desperately wanted to remain faithful.

_____

_____

We, as could Peter, can take comfort knowing that through every trial, in spite of all our mistakes, and during every temptation, we are not abandoned by our Lord. He disciplines, but He doesn't abandon.

Application for Day Three

We are never abandoned by Jesus. What better proof of that fact than His decision to appear to Peter before any of the other disciples! Peter was an eyewitness to the majesty of Christ—His splendor, His glory, His Power, and His magnificent love.

In 2 Peter 1:16, what did Peter say he witnessed?

_____

The Greek word translated "majesty" in this verse is *magaleiotes*. The word means "superbness; i.e., glory or splendor: magnificence, majesty, mighty power." There is another Greek word translated "majesty" in the NIV: *megalosune*. It means "greatness; i.e., divinity (often God himself), majesty." Jesus was without a doubt divine and great, but Peter chose to use a word that focuses on the "superbness" of Jesus. Jesus was, above all, excellent, of highest quality. Jesus exuded supreme splendor, glory, and power. Jesus loved with an excellent, pure love.

Through Peter's use of the word "majesty," he attempted to convey everything he had witnessed as Jesus' close follower, including the brilliant and glorious image he saw standing before him at the Transfiguration—a preview of the glory we will one day see as we stand before our Lord, face-to-face.

Application for Day Four

As Peter finished breakfast by the lake, I wonder if he paused for a moment to reflect.

Re-read John 21:15–19.

Peter was sitting beside the very body of water where he had worked as a fisherman. It was the same sea where he first experienced Jesus' miraculous power, briefly walked on the water, and saw Jesus calm a furious storm.

As the memories flooded his mind, did Peter's heart swell with gratitude? Did he glance one last time at the fishing boat he'd left behind? As he turned away to follow Jesus, I imagine Peter knew his life would never be the same.

That morning by the lake was a pivotal moment in Peter's life. Have you had a moment (or moments) in your life when you knew things would never again be the same? If so, describe the circumstances and some of the emotions you experienced:

_____

_____

_____

The humbling day at the seashore gave way to a glorious day of worship and praise. Next week, we'll get our first glimpse of Peter as the Rock Jesus knew he would one day become! I pray you are encouraged as you too strive to be everything you were created to be.

WEEK SEVEN

141

Week 8

Enlightening Revelations

Firstfruits

*Not only so, but we ourselves, who have the firstfruits of the Spirit,
groan inwardly as we wait eagerly for our adoption as sons,
the redemption of our bodies.*

ROMANS 8:23

Up to this point in the study, we've traveled with Peter as an eyewitness to the life of Jesus. Last week we studied Jesus' trial, crucifixion, and resurrection, then Peter's restoration by the Sea of Galilee. Today, we will look at what I think is an interesting correlation between the Jewish festivals of the Passover season and the dates of the Crucifixion, Jesus' resurrection, and the arrival of the promised Holy Spirit.

Let's begin by reading Acts 1:1–13.

According to verses 4 and 5, what were the apostles instructed to wait for in Jerusalem?

Now read Acts 2:1–4.

What day did the apostles see Jesus' words come to pass?

Pentecost is the Greek name for the Jewish celebration called _Shavuot_, or "Feast of Weeks."[39] There is great significance in the Holy Spirit's arrival on this day, and to fully understand it, we need to take a look at several of the festivals of the Passover season. Of course, the season began with the Passover Meal itself, celebrated on the fourteenth day of Nissan, the first month of the Hebrew calendar. Study the chart below and keep in mind, Hebrew days begin and end at sundown.

NISSAN[40]						
Sun	Mon	Tues	Wed	Thurs	Fri	Sat
						1
2	3	4	5	6	7	8
9	10	11	12	13	14 PASSOVER	15 SABBATH
16 FIRSTFRUITS	17	18	19	20	21	22
23	24	25	26	27	28	29
30						

The Passover began at sundown on the thirteenth day of Nissan, so Jesus would have eaten the Passover Meal with His disciples that Thursday evening. Jesus, as the ultimate Passover Lamb, was crucified around noon (Luke 23:44) on Friday, the 14th (still Passover), and His body was placed in the tomb before sundown. The third day began at sunset on Saturday, the 15th (refer to the calendar above). The morning of the 16th (still the third day), Jesus rose from the dead.

Look again at the calendar. On what Jewish holiday was Jesus resurrected?

Firstfruits marked the beginning of the grain harvests in Israel. A sheaf of barley was harvested and brought to the temple as a thanksgiving offering to the Lord for the harvest. This offering was called the Firstfruits Offering. Most importantly, it was representative of the barley harvest as a whole and served as a pledge, or guarantee, that the remainder of the harvest would be realized in the days that followed.[41]

> Jesus was the Firstfruit of the harvest of souls!

Now read Revelation 14:14–16.

Jesus was the Firstfruit of the harvest of souls! His resurrection is the pledge, or guarantee, that we too will be resurrected to eternal life at the final harvest of souls when Jesus returns.

Now the day of Pentecost took place on the fiftieth day after Firstfruits. This day was set aside for the Jewish people to give a free-will offering of grain from the firstfruits of their final grain harvest of the season, which was the wheat harvest. The day of Pentecost was also the beginning of Jewish Feast of Weeks. The Talmud and Josephus referred to the Feast of Weeks as *Atzeret*, meaning "conclusion." Jews viewed the Feast of Weeks as the conclusion of the Passover season and of the seven-week spring harvest.[42]

With these celebrations in mind, let's take a peek at the conclusion of the harvest of souls. Please read Revelation 21:1–5.

Everything will be made new! These passages are some of my very favorite in all of Scripture because they remind us of what awaits us for eternity. My heart yearns for the day when all believers in Christ will see these events come to pass.

Read Romans 8:18–25.

What firstfruits does verse 23 indicate we (as believers in Christ) have?

_____

Read 2 Corinthians 5:4–5. Summarize these verses in your own words:

_____

_____

_____

All Creation longs for the day when it will be made new again. Believers in Christ have received the gift of the Holy Spirit, which is the Firstfruit of the Spirit. Our spirits groan inwardly as we await that glorious day when we will see the ultimate fulfillment of God's pledge at the final harvest of souls.

The correlation between the Jewish festivals of the Passover season and Jesus' crucifixion, His resurrection, and the first indwelling of the Holy Spirit confirm the truth that our God is a God of perfect order. Nothing is by happenstance. We can take comfort in God's sovereignty.

> All Creation longs for the day when it will be made new again.

Tomorrow we will watch as Peter and the apostles begin to grasp the power and authority they were granted through the Holy Spirit. We will witness a few events in Peter's budding ministry and watch as he is transformed by the power of the Spirit.

WEEK EIGHT | DAY TWO

Chip off the Old Rock

As you come to Him, the living Stone—rejected by men but chosen by God and precious to Him—you also, like living stones, are being built into a spiritual house to be a holy priesthood, offering spiritual sacrifices acceptable to God through Jesus Christ.

1 PETER 2:4–5

Earlier in our study, we saw Jesus' compassion as He lovingly rebuked, and then restored, Peter by the Sea of Galilee. Peter may not have stood near the cross, but he was deeply impacted by Jesus' death. He ran, probably shoving his way past the less impulsive disciple John, to see the empty tomb. Peter leapt into the water and swam to meet Jesus by the sea.

When we last saw Peter, he and the other disciples had just received the gift of the Holy Spirit. Let's see what happened next.

Begin by reading Acts 2:5–41.

How many were added to their number that day? _____

Did that bold man, passionately preaching the gospel, sound like the same Peter who distanced Himself from Jesus and denied Him three times? Not a trace of that fearful man was evident to the crowd in Jerusalem that day!

According to verse 38, what did Peter urge the people to do?

_____

Jesus had told the disciples before He ascended to heaven this would happen.

Read Luke 24:44–49.

Peter was clothed with power from the Holy Spirit and preached the gospel for the first time in Jerusalem, just as Jesus said. The difference so evident in Peter was the indwelling of the Holy Spirit.

> Peter was clothed with power from the Holy Spirit and preached the gospel for the first time in Jerusalem, just as Jesus said.

Look back at Matthew 16:16–18.

In Week Four we discussed the fact that the church would be built on the rock (Petra—mass of rock, which is Christ) and that Peter (Petros) would be one of the many pieces brought together with Jesus to make that foundation. Peter was the first to claim his destiny as a "chip off the old Rock" of Jesus Christ. But guess what? As a believer, you too are a piece of the rock upon which Jesus is building His church. Let's see how Peter explained it.

Please read 1 Peter 2:4–5.

You, as a living stone, are part of the spiritual house of Jesus Christ. What kind of sacrifices are we to make as members of that spiritual house, according to verse 5?

_____

Now read Hebrews 13:15–16.

What are some spiritual sacrifices we can make that please God?

_____

_____

Let's discuss each of these spiritual sacrifices. First, praise. Jesus Christ was the atoning blood sacrifice. All sins have been covered by His blood. We have salvation and cleansing through that blood, and there is nothing we can do to earn it. It is a gift. But we can offer our Lord the one thing He cannot give Himself: PRAISE!

Praise is any word or deed that exalts or honors God. We give God praise when we exalt and honor Him in the eyes of others. Some Hebrew words, such as "towdah", for instance, are often translated "praise" in our Bibles, but can also be translated "thanksgiving."

> Praise is any word or deed that exalts or honors God.

Take a moment to thank God by noting something specific He has done in your life recently.

_____

_____

Peter was offering praise to God by exalting Him before the crowd gathered in Jerusalem. He honored and exalted God by making known what God had done through Jesus Christ. I am quite sure God was pleased with the sacrifice offered up by Peter in Jerusalem that day. Watch for opportunities to offer up a sacrifice of praise to our Lord.

Next, let's talk about the spiritual sacrifice of sharing with others. When we give to others in Jesus' name, we bring honor and glory to God. It is a spiritual sacrifice that I would guess brings a smile to His holy face. Through acts of benevolence, we make Jesus evident to believers and non-believers alike. Have you ever awakened in the morning with a person on your mind? Or maybe you find yourself continually thinking about the struggle a friend is facing. I encourage you to respond when God lays someone on your heart. That person may be praying for just exactly what you have to give, be it encouragement, clothing, food, or possibly money. When you act in response to God's prompting and give as He directs, He is glorified in the process.

Has there been a time in your life when someone made Jesus real to you through an act of kindness or by filling a need in your life? If so, write a brief description of the situation:

_____

_____

_____

Now let's explore the spiritual sacrifice of doing good. Let's see what Peter had to say on the subject.

Please read 1 Peter 2:4–12.

According to verse 12, what is the result of our good deeds?

_____

We do good deeds to glorify God, not to earn favor with Him. Our behavior doesn't earn points and we cannot manipulate our Creator into doing what we ask of Him. There is nothing we can do to earn our salvation. Our motive for doing good deeds should be to bring glory to God, to exalt Him in the eyes of others, and to ultimately bring people around us into a saving relationship with Jesus Christ.

Peter's ultimate purpose for saying everything he said as he addressed the crowd in Jerusalem was simple.

Re-read Acts 2:36–41.

Peter preached in order that the people present might "save [them]selves" through repentance and belief in Jesus as the Christ.

According to Luke 5:31–32, why did Jesus come to Earth as a man?

_____

> Our motive for doing good deeds should be to bring glory to God, to exalt Him in the eyes of others, and to ultimately bring people around us into a saving relationship with Jesus Christ.

WEEK EIGHT

Peter was indeed a chip off the old Rock. He was like the living stone. Peter began his ministry offering spiritual sacrifices to God by sharing the message of salvation with those in Jerusalem on that blustery afternoon when the Holy Spirit blew in and clothed him with power from on high. The result? Three thousand were added to the spiritual house that day.

WEEK EIGHT | DAY THREE

Participating in Suffering

But rejoice that you participate in the sufferings of Christ,
so that you may be overjoyed when his glory is revealed.

1 PETER 4:13

The apostles continued to preach, and God continued to add to their numbers daily. The religious leaders didn't know what to do. They even brought Peter and John before the Sanhedrin (the supreme court and administrative body of the Jews) and commanded them to stop preaching and teaching in Jesus' name. They threatened Peter and John strongly and then released them, unsure what else to do with them.

Peter and John then went back to the community of believers and told them all that was said. Rather than succumb to the threats, the determined group of believers prayed and asked God to enable them to speak His Word with greater boldness. God answered their prayer, even shook the very ground where they stood, and all the believers were filled

> Rather than succumb to the threats, the determined group of believers prayed and asked God to enable them to speak His Word with greater boldness.

with the Holy Spirit. The enthusiastic followers began to declare God's Word fearlessly. The apostles continued performing miracles and healing the sick. Crowds gathered from surrounding towns, bringing their sick to be healed.

Please read Acts 5:17–32.

According to verse 28, what orders had Peter and John been given by the Sanhedrin?

_____

Paraphrase the words of the apostles to the Sanhedrin as recorded in verse 32.

_____

_____

_____

I find it incredible that modern believers, two thousand years after Jesus walked this earth, can testify as witnesses to the message of the gospel through the power of the Holy Spirit. The apostles felt compelled to share the message of Jesus Christ because they were indeed eyewitnesses to what they preached. We obviously can't see with our eyes, but we can experience the risen Savior through His Holy Spirit. As we experience the presence and activity of our Lord through His Spirit, we too come to the point we can't keep it to ourselves!

> We obviously can't see with our eyes, but we can experience the risen Savior through His Holy Spirit.

Now read Acts 5:33–42.

Write Peter's words as recorded in Acts 5:29.

_____

Depending on the version of your Bible, you may get the impression Peter angrily responded to the rebuke by the religious leaders. However, in the original Greek, these verses read more like, "Peter and the apostles said: it behooves us to obey God rather than men"[43] in a firm, yet respectful tone. The apostles willingly submitted to the officers to face the court, but their first loyalty was to God and Peter respectfully refused to disobey Jesus' command to preach the gospel.

Why did the apostles rejoice, according to verse 41?

His appearance before the Sanhedrin was an illustration of submitting to authorities while maintaining our loyalty and commitment to Jesus.

We can learn so much from Peter. He and the other apostles were flogged before being released, yet they didn't resist or bitterly lash out at their abusers. Let's read a little of what Peter had to say about submitting to authorities and suffering because of Christ.

Please read 1 Peter 2:13–25.

What did Peter say is commendable for believers in Christ (vs. 20-21)?

The apostles were doing a good work by spreading the gospel. They endured the flogging and Peter was able to rejoice because he and his partners in ministry shared in Christ's suffering.

Now read 1 Peter 4:12–19.

Peter and the apostles faced persecution continually from the Jewish community. The churches who received Peter's letter had experienced horrific punishment for their faith. Most of us will never be flogged. As a matter of fact, many of us have never really experienced intense persecution for our faith. But there are areas around our globe where Christians are in danger of death or torture every day because they follow Jesus.

> Many of us have never really experienced intense persecution for our faith. But there are areas around our globe where Christians are in danger of death or torture every day because they follow Jesus.

In the fall of 2000, I had the privilege of serving on a team who offered a women's Bible study for Sudanese refugees. These were some of the warmest, sweetest women I had ever met. Nothing could have prepared me for the stories these women told of their lives in Sudan. *The New Foxe's Book of Martyrs* has this to say of persecution in Sudan:

> During the past thirty years, about three million people have been killed in Sudan because of their religious beliefs—particularly Christians or members of animist religions—according to Ulrich Delius, an expert on Africa from the German Society

for Endangered Peoples. In 1989, Sudan was taken over by Muslim extremists and declared an Islamic state. In 1992, the military junta in Khartoum declared 'holy war' against non-Muslims. Government soldiers have committed massacres among the civilian population. "Soldiers plunder the villages, rape the women, and torture or kill the men," said Delius.[44]

The women I met and studied with had experienced persecution and suffering in ways I can't even imagine. One woman described hiding friends in the backseat of her car, buried in coal, in order to sneak them out of the country. Had she been caught, she said she would have been tortured and/or killed. Another woman had watched as her sister was brutally murdered. Many of these women were haunted by guilt, shame, and pain. Some of them had loved ones still in Sudan. We prayed often for the women to find peace, including an end to their nightmares.

Coming from a middle-class American home, I felt ill-equipped to minister to these women. They had lived in such intense persecution and hardship while in Sudan that their meager government housing here seemed a safe harbor of luxury in comparison. They felt safe. Yet I, along with three other women who were leading the study, required a man acting as a bodyguard to accompany us to and from the property. It was truly a humbling experience. I still pray for the women whenever God brings them to mind. Their stories and their courage have impacted me greatly.

Most of us will never face that type of persecution. It amazes me how much difficulty we Americans have just sharing our faith with a store clerk or a co-worker. Yet people in other countries would rather die than keep quiet.

Peter said, "Rejoice that you participate in the sufferings of Christ, so that you may be overjoyed when his glory is revealed" (1 Peter 4:13). What are some ways we can participate in the sufferings of Christ?

_____

_____

_____

_____

One way we can participate in the sufferings of Christ is to share our faith, even when we are uncomfortable or risking rejection.

WEEK EIGHT

There is another significant way we can participate, and that is to pray for those suffering because of their faith in Jesus. Consider designating fifteen minutes of your prayer time each week to praying for those being persecuted around the world. I suggest picking up a copy of the *The New Foxe's Book of Martyrs*. The book contains a whole section on martyrs in the past century. Read through testimonials for a particular country and pray for Christians enduring persecution there. There are a number of organizations, many with Web sites, who offer information about countries where persecution of Christians is a regular occurrence.

Whatever the method, prayer is one way we can participate in the suffering of the body of Christ. God is the only One who can change the hearts of those persecuting Christians around the world. He is the only One who can bring peace. You may never be called upon to suffer physically for the sake of Christ, but you can participate by praying for those who are.

> There are a number of organizations, many with Web sites, who offer information about countries where persecution of Christians is a regular occurrence.

WEEK EIGHT | DAY FOUR

Divine Orchestration

While Peter was wondering about the meaning of the vision, the men sent by Cornelius found out where Simon's house was and stopped at the gate.

ACTS 10:17

After the apostles were flogged and released, the church continued to grow. With that growth came stronger persecution. The persecution became so intense the Jews even began to kill Christians, beginning with the notorious stoning of Stephen. Christians scattered throughout the region. Peter and John traveled to some of these areas performing miracles and healing the sick. Many more believed and the church continued to grow larger and larger in spite of the persecution.

As we begin our lesson today, we'll find Peter in Joppa, staying with a tanner named Simon.

Please read Acts 10:1–22.

One of my favorite terms for God's activity is "divine orchestration." It describes God manipulating circumstances in order to carry out His plan. The text we just read is a wonderful example. The centurion received instructions about Peter, and Peter received instructions that prepared him to accept the invitation to visit Cornelius. Both "visions" were delivered with precise timing.

> One of my favorite terms for God's activity is "divine orchestration."

God works that way in our lives today, too. The key to recognizing His activity is prayer.

At what time of day did Cornelius see his vision (v. 3)? _____

According to Acts 3:1, what was significant about this time of day?

_____

_____

Why did Peter go up onto the roof at noon (Acts 10:9)? _____

These men were both praying when they received their instructions from God. Often we fail to see God's activity in our lives because we lack the discipline of regular prayer time with God.

Read Psalm 55:17 (written by King David) and Daniel 6:10.

What did David and Daniel have in common?

_____

King David and Daniel were both used mightily by God, and they were both in the habit of praying three times a day. Now I'm not suggesting that we all stop and have prayer time three times a day or become legalistic about the discipline of prayer, but I do believe a regular prayer time is important if you want to experience God's presence, hear His voice, and participate in His activity.

Please read Acts 10:23–48.

WEEK EIGHT

Peter and Cornelius each received a message straight from God, and they both responded. Peter left with the soldiers without hesitation, just as God had asked him to.

What question did Peter ask of Cornelius in verse 29?

_____

_____

Is that not amazing?! Peter left with the men sent by Cornelius even though it was against Jewish law to associate with Gentiles, and he went without even knowing why! Peter was told by the Spirit not to hesitate and he obeyed, without objection, without question.

That, my sister in Christ, is the same Spirit we have living in us and the same Spirit that prompts us to act. Yet, how often do we hesitate to do far less than take a two-day journey to meet with strangers without knowing why we're going?

And Cornelius? According to verse 24, what did Cornelius do before the soldiers returned with Peter?

_____

_____

_____

Cornelius was so sure Peter would come that he called together his relatives and close friends. He had them come over to his house to hear what Peter had to say. That is faith.

Look again at verses 27 and 28.

Cornelius was well aware it was against the Jewish law for Peter to come and associate with Gentiles. Yet, he was firmly convinced Peter would come. Can you imagine what some people must have said when Cornelius invited them to his house to hear from a Jew? It must have sounded ridiculous. But Cornelius was so sure Peter would show up that he was able to convince a large gathering of people to come. His faith must have been inspiring.

> Cornelius was well aware it was against the Jewish law for Peter to come and associate with Gentiles. Yet, he was firmly convinced Peter would come.

What do you think made the people come to Cornelius's house that day?

_____

_____

_____

_____

I believe it was, at least in part, his enthusiasm. Have you ever been around people who are so excited about what they are doing that some of that excitement spills over and you just want to join them? Cornelius had seen an angel and received an audible message from God. Nothing is more exciting than experiencing divine orchestration!

Take a moment to thank God for this example in Scripture of His work. I encourage you to watch for that same divinely orchestrated work in your own life.

WEEK EIGHT DAY FIVE

Personal Application

Application for Day One

On Day One we explored the correlation between the timing of Jewish festivals and the events of Christ's crucifixion, His resurrection, and the arrival of the Holy Spirit. The final harvest of souls will take place when Jesus returns. Until that day, we believers are called to live in a manner that honors God. Today, we will look briefly at what Peter had to say about the lifestyle we are called to lead as we wait.

Please read 1 Peter 4:1–11.

Verse 4 says, "They [non-believers] think it is strange that you do not plunge with them into the same flood of dissipation [indulgence] and they heap abuse on you." You may not relate to these passages. However, for those of us who as adults came to know Jesus, this passage has a familiar ring.

I accepted Jesus as my Savior when I was twenty-six years old. Because I had taken a few swims in the flood of indulgence along the way, I had to distance myself from a few old friends and make a dramatic change in my lifestyle. I had a little abuse heaped upon me, as Peter would say.

How about you? Whether you grew up attending church or you came to know Jesus as an adult, at some point in your life you probably had to make some changes in order to "live according to God in regard to the Spirit." What changes have you made?

_____

_____

_____

_____

Peter tells us that the end of all things is near and that we should be clear-minded and self-controlled so we can pray. What does Peter say we should do "above all," according to verse 8?

_____

The Greek word translated "deeply" is *ektenes.* It was used to describe the taut muscles of an athlete who strains to win a race.[45]

I ran cross-country track in elementary and middle school. Trust me, I am familiar with the taut muscles of one straining to win a race. As a matter of fact, I did far more straining than winning. Those last few meters of a race were often quite painful. I had to push my short legs hard to keep up with the long-legged runners around me. Had determination and effort won the race, I'd have placed every time. Effort and determination (and yes, pain) are required to "love deeply." We must strain and stretch with everything we have to love someone with the kind of love Peter describes in this passage.

> Effort and determination (and yes, pain) are required to "love deeply."

This kind of love doesn't expose the faults of others. It covers them up. It walks away when the latest on So-and-So's struggle becomes the conversation after Bible study. It finds the good in someone who is difficult or grumpy. This kind of love is painful at times. Yet Peter tells us, "above all," love until it hurts.

Re-read 1 Peter 4:9–11. How do we show love to others in the body of Christ?

_____

_____

_____

Ask God to help you love until it hurts, so in all things God may be praised through Jesus Christ.

Application for Day Two

On Day Two we learned that we believers, like living stones, are being built into a spiritual house, which is the church. As such, we should offer spiritual sacrifices acceptable to God. To refresh your memory, re-read Hebrews 13:15–16 and note the spiritual sacrifices that please God.

_____

_____

Sharing with others and doing good are among those spiritual sacrifices. Not only do we cover a multitude of sins when we love deeply—we please God. We all have a person in our lives whom we find difficult to love. Whether this person is a family member, a co-worker, or someone who sits in a pew near you every Sunday morning, it pleases God when you do good, share with her, and serve her.

> Not only do we cover a multitude of sins when we love deeply—we please God.

Write a prayer committing to love this person deeply by serving her and covering sins with grace and mercy such as you've received from God:

_____

_____

WEEK EIGHT

_____

_____

_____

Application for Day Three

On Day Three we talked about participating in the suffering of the church through prayer. Well, I wouldn't want to change the theme of our lesson today midstream, so let's put a prayerful twist on our commitment to love our "difficult person" deeply.

I encourage you to pray for your "difficult person" every day for the next two weeks. Avoid the usual "Lord, please change her!" prayers. Instead, pray for her well-being and her relationship with God. To get you started, I've included a few Scripture passage you can personalize as you pray. (Be careful! You just might be someone else's "difficult person.")

Psalm 25:4–7   Psalm 1:1–3   Psalm 67:1–2

Application for Day Four

On Day Four we witnessed "divine orchestration" as God worked in the lives of Cornelius and Peter to accomplish His purpose of offering salvation to the Gentiles.

Write Romans 8:28 in your own words:

_____

_____

_____

Have you ever considered that God may have placed your "difficult person" in your path in order to work good in *you*, as well as your "difficult person's" life? Sometimes that woman who really pushes your buttons or brings out the worst in you is part of God's plan to refine you and mold you more fully into the image of His Son. Divine orchestration is not always pleasant, but it is always for the greater good.

Please read James 1:2–4.

Okay, you know where I'm going with this by now, I'm sure. It is possible your "difficult person" is in your life to help you develop perseverance.

According to verse 4, what purpose might God have for causing you to develop perseverance?

_____

_____

As a way of closing today's lesson, spend a few minutes in prayer, thanking God for the "difficult person" in your life. Ask God to reveal your own weaknesses as you react to this person. As you do, He will cause you to become a little more mature and complete. And if you continue to persevere, eventually you will not lack anything. Glory to God!

WEEK EIGHT

Week 9

Refining Encounters

Golden Freedom

*Suddenly an angel of the Lord appeared and a light shone in the cell.
He struck Peter on the side and woke him up. "Quick, get up!" he said,
and the chains fell off Peter's wrists.*

ACTS 12:7

After Peter first preached the gospel to Gentiles at the home of Cornelius, others began to preach to Gentiles in Antioch, where believers were first given the name "Christians."

Please read Acts 12:1–19.

Peter lay captive between two soldiers, bound with chains. But the Lord brought light to Peter's dark prison cell, broke the chains that bound him, and set him free.

That is exactly what Christ does for us spiritually. Without Christ we are captive to sin and our sinful natures. But if we choose to get up and follow Him, our chains fall off and we are led to freedom in Christ. We are free from the law of sin and death, free to live hopeful and abundant lives here on Earth so we look forward to the day we will be free to live in heaven with our Savior for all eternity.

But freedom in Christ does not mean freedom from trials. So how do we live in freedom while enduring the hardships of this life?

Please read 1 Peter 1:1–7.

Trials reveal the depth of our faith. We find out what we truly believe when our circumstances get tough. Our faith is strengthened through struggles if we hold on tightly to God.

> Trials reveal the depth of our faith.

During times of trial, when we ask God to grow our faith, what is the result, according to verse 7?

_____

_____

_____

Our faith brings God glory! We often seek to glorify God through our works, but Peter tells us that our faith—of greater worth than gold—also brings God glory, honor, and praise.

Now read 1 Peter 1:8–12.

The prophets were not speaking on their own or for themselves. They were speaking under the inspiration of the Holy Spirit, so our faith in Christ could be confirmed through the Word of God, which we each hold in our hands. Scripture is not simply a collection of ancient writings. The Bible contains divinely inspired words that applied to the Christians of Peter's day and apply to each and every one of us today.

Our faith is based on the divinely inspired Word of God, not on the wisdom of men or the philosophies or riches of the world, which perish and fade. We are called to live by faith, according to the Word. In our next reading, Peter tells us exactly how to do that.

Please read 1 Peter 1:13–21.

We are called to prepare our minds for action by being self-controlled and by living holy and pure lives.

Read Romans 12:1–2 and note the link between living a holy and pure life and preparing one's mind for action.

_____

_____

_____

We live holy and pure lives by allowing the Word of God to transform us into the image of Jesus Christ. The more time we spend in the Word, the less we will be conformed to the beliefs and actions of the world around us and the more our thoughts and actions will reflect Jesus. And Romans 12:2 tells us that as we are transformed, we are better able to know and do the will of God.

> We live holy and pure lives by allowing the Word of God to transform us into the image of Jesus Christ.

Now read 1 Peter 1:22–25.

Our lives change as we obey God's Word and that change should be revealed in the way we relate to our brothers and sisters in Christ. We spent a lot of time last week on the subject of loving one another "deeply." Jesus told us that the greatest of all God's commandments is to love God. It is our profound love for God (along with His for us) that enables us to express deep love for others. By continuing to foster an intimate relationship with God, our relationships with our family members, co-workers, and friends will become richer and healthier as well. One way we develop an intimate relationship with our Lord is by studying His Word.

Re-read 1 Peter 1:24–25. Restate these verses in your own words below.

_____

_____

_____

This passage reminds me of a poem I memorized as a teenager. Take a moment to read it before we go on.

WEEK NINE

Nothing Gold Can Stay

by Robert Frost

Nature's first green is gold,

Her hardest hue to hold.

Her early leaf's a flower;

But only so an hour.

Then leaf subsides to leaf.

So Eden sank to grief,

So dawn goes down to day.

Nothing gold can stay.

The fall of man in the Garden of Eden made all mankind prisoners to the law of sin and death. This poem eloquently states the futility of trying to maintain our innocence on our own. If we place our faith and trust in *people,* we will be disappointed. In this world, apart from Christ, we are as incapable of maintaining the fresh and beautiful innocence of a child as nature is incapable of maintaining the freshness and beauty of a flower.

What does Peter tell us lasts forever (v. 25)?

> If we place our faith and trust in *people,* we will be disappointed.

Now read 1 Peter 2:1–3.

We have been born again through Christ, and, through the power of the Holy Spirit, we can rid ourselves of deceitful, ungodly behavior. We have the power to remain "gold," pure and holy. But we need to nourish ourselves on the "pure spiritual milk" of God's Word. That is how we get up, walk by faith, and follow God to the blessed realization of golden freedom in Christ.

Counseled Council

For it seemed good to the Holy Ghost, and to us, to lay upon you no greater burden than these necessary things.

ACTS 15:28 KJV

After Peter's miraculous escape from prison, he "left for another place." Persecution against Christians continued to increase. But something even more destructive began to plague the early church—division.

Some of the Jewish Christians began trying to impose circumcision, required by Jewish law, on the new Gentile believers. They started teaching that in addition to placing one's faith in Jesus, Gentiles needed to be circumcised in order to be saved.

According to Ephesians 2:8, what saves us?

_____

_____

Peter knew circumcision was not required. He had been the first to preach to the Gentiles at the home of Cornelius. He had watched as those Gentiles received a visible manifestation of the Holy Spirit. Yet, as we will see in our next reading, Peter struggled when these misguided Jewish Christians arrived in Antioch.

> Peter ate freely with the Gentile believers, knowing they were one through their faith in Jesus Christ.

Begin by reading Galatians 2:11–16.

Before these misled Jewish Christians arrived, Peter ate freely with the Gentile believers, knowing they were one through their faith in Jesus Christ. But when the Jewish Christians began to oppose the Gentiles openly, Peter wavered. My guess is the waning of Peter's convictions happened slowly, with Peter fellowshipping more and more with the Jews at meals and drawing back from the Gentiles' tables. Regardless of how it actually happened, Peter's actions led to outright division among the community of believers.

What insight do you gain on this subject from Galatians 3:26–28?

_____

_____

_____

Peter must have handled Paul's rebuke pretty well, but this confrontation was a pivotal moment in Peter's ministry as well as Paul's. Let's see how the situation was resolved.

Please read Galatians 2:9–10.

Peter had been the first to preach to the Gentiles, but his primary ministry would be to the Jews. Peter agreed to preach to the Jews and Paul would preach to the Gentiles. Although the confrontation with Paul was probably extremely uncomfortable for Peter, the situation gave Peter clarity about where his primary focus in ministry should be at that time.

> Peter had been the first to preach to the Gentiles, but his primary ministry would be to the Jews.

Sometimes, like Peter, we have to stumble and fall a bit in order to discover our true passions and get clarity about our specific ministries. Have you ever failed as you attempted to serve in a particular area of ministry in your church? If so, briefly describe the circumstances and the lessons you learned through the experience:

_____

_____

_____

_____

Although the two strong leaders of the early church reconciled and moved on, the division within the church did not end with their confrontation. A little while later, Peter got an opportunity to set the record straight himself. Let's take a look at what he said.

Please read Acts 15:1–11.

Peter boldly addressed the council. We are all saved by grace through faith in Jesus Christ, he asserted, not by works, or by devotion. This is interesting reading. Let's see how the council handled this difficult situation!

Read Acts 15:12–35.

The council, by the direction of the Holy Spirit, sent a formal letter, releasing Gentiles from the burden of the Jewish law. What insight into some of their reasoning do you gain from verse 19?

_____

_____

_____

> Sometimes we in the church make life difficult for new believers.

Sometimes we in the church make life difficult for new believers. We get focused on changing them, trying to make them conform to our model of a "good" Christian. We need to be careful not to overburden new believers with legalistic rules. If we'll love them, teach them, and care for their needs, the Holy Spirit of God will do the changing. And He's far better at transforming a life than any of us will ever be.

Please re-read Peter's words in Acts 15:10.

How can you relate the warning in this passage to the church of today? (For additional insight, read Luke 6:41–42 and Romans 3:21–24.)

_____

_____

_____

WEEK NINE

_____

_____

We all fall short and we all have sinned (Romans 3:23). When new believers come into the body of Christ, we should shower them with God's love and grace as we gently help them connect with growing believers and mercifully teach the truths of God's Word. Our goal should be to guide them to the Word and allow the Word and the Holy Spirit to do the convicting. There are times when we need to confront a brother or sister in Christ, but I believe those times are few, and we need to be sure it is God prompting us to confront, not our own pride or legalism.

Peter and the other leaders of the early church came to the conclusion, through the leading of the Holy Spirit, that it was not good to burden with unnecessary rules and regulations those putting their trust in God.

What did Jesus say the role of the Holy Spirit is, according to John 14:26?

_____

_____

_____

_____

_____

A counselor is one who advises and provides guidance. I love the way the Holy Spirit is mentioned as an active member of the council. "It seemed good to the Holy Spirit and to us . . ." I would say this was a counseled council!

Unfading Beauty

Your beauty should not come from outward adornment, such as braided hair and the wearing of gold jewelry and fine clothes. Instead, it should be that of your inner self, the unfading beauty of a gentle and quiet spirit, which is of great worth in God's sight.

1 PETER 3:3–4

For eight weeks we've traveled with Peter as an eyewitness to the majesty of Christ. We watched as the early church was established. We saw Peter stumble, and we saw him succeed. We watched as Peter was transformed from Simon, the ordinary fisherman, to Peter, fisher of men. We've cried with Peter, and we've gotten a laugh or two at his expense. But from this point forward in our study, Peter will be our teacher. He was schooled by the Master Himself. He learned many lessons and became a faithful shepherd to the early church, just as His Lord had commissioned him to do. We can learn a lot from Simon Peter.

> From this point forward in our study, Peter will be our teacher.

Today Peter's lesson is specifically addressed to women. The message is about true beauty—the unfading beauty of a gentle and quiet spirit.

Please begin by reading 1 Peter 3:1–2.

Peter's words may make your spine stiffen, but let's take these passages apart in order to clearly understand Peter's point.

According to verse 1, to whom are women to submit?

Not all men, but to their own husbands. Why?

_____

_____

Before we continue, please re-read 1 Peter 2:13, 18.

Peter says that in the same way that we submit to worldly authorities for the Lord's sake, and that slaves submit to their masters with all respect, we are to submit to our husbands, whether they are believers or not.

Peter indicated that our submissive behavior would silence those who are critical of Christians. Just as we submit to our government authorities in order to have order and structure in society, our submission to our husbands will help maintain order in our homes. But the greatest benefit of our submission is the effect it will have on our husbands.

My heart breaks for those of you whose husbands are not believers. I know you have a difficult walk, and as much as I'd like to, I can't fully understand your struggles. But I know that you have hope through Jesus Christ. If you are one of the many women who sit alone in a pew on Sunday mornings year after year, be encouraged by Peter's words. Your husband may never have walked through the doors of a church, but he can be impacted by your "walk" in your home. I want to caution you, though. Remember, the walking is your responsibility, but the impacting is God's. Don't try to do His part or you'll undermine yours.

> If you are one of the many women who sit alone in a pew on Sunday mornings year after year, be encouraged by Peter's words.

Now read 1 Peter 3:3–4.

What does Peter tell us in verse 4 is of great worth to God?

_____

Let's look at each of these characteristics separately. First, a gentle spirit. The Greek word translated "gentle" in this verse is *praus*. It means "mild, by implication humble; meek." This word is used in another passage I think you will find familiar.

Please read Matthew 21:1–5.

Jesus humbly entered Jerusalem on the back of a donkey. He was the King of kings. He was the Son of God. Yet He entered the city in a modest manner. Having a gentle spirit doesn't make you weaker than those around you. As a matter of fact, gentleness conveys an inner strength few people are able to attain. To be humble and gentle with others, you have to be at peace with yourself. Jesus knew He was the King and the Son of God. The way He entered the city didn't matter.

Regardless of how others treat you, my precious sister in Christ, nothing can change who you are, or whose you are. As you develop a gentle spirit, you are displaying the spirit of your Lord and Savior.

What does Romans 8:29 tell you?

_____

_____

Reflecting the spirit of Jesus is your ultimate purpose in life! It is your destiny.

Now let's take a look at the Greek word translated "quiet" in 1 Peter 3:4. It is *hesuchia*, and I think you will be surprised by its meaning. It is defined as "keeping one's seat (sedentary), by implication still (undisturbed, undisturbing); peaceable, quiet."

The word simply implies we know our place—we don't cause trouble or jump in where we don't belong. I don't mean to meddle, but in what ways can you display a quiet spirit as you relate to your husband?

_____

_____

_____

_____

In our marriages, we need to know our place. Peter wasn't saying we shouldn't speak up at all, but we need to know when to speak up and when to be still. We have to know when to correct our husbands and when to keep our mouths shut. I hope you hear my heart on this, but I believe it is a rare situation when it is acceptable for a woman to correct her husband in front of others. When women correct their husbands while they are telling a story or making a

> I hope you hear my heart on this, but I believe it is a rare situation when it is acceptable for a woman to correct her husband in front of others.

WEEK NINE

statement, it undermines their husband's credibility and communicates disrespect. Let's face it, unless someone will be harmed by the mistake, it's more important for our husbands to feel respected than for their stories or statements to be perfectly accurate.

By "keeping our seats" when our husbands talk, we show our support, and cause others to respect them as well. I encourage you to communicate with your husband to help determine your place within your marriage. You and your husband have different strengths and weaknesses. A good, open discussion, where you both define your roles and responsibilities, can be a great way to foster better communication and cooperation within your marriage relationship. By defining roles and boundaries, you will have a better sense of when to speak up and when to keep your seat.

There is nothing more beautiful than a woman with a gentle and quiet spirit. This kind of beauty doesn't fade when you remove your makeup in the evening. It is steadfast regardless of your economic situation. An "unfading beauty" is of great value to God. I don't know a woman alive who doesn't want her husband to consider her beautiful. But no matter how physically attractive one might be as a young woman, some day that youthful beauty will fade. However, a gentle and quiet spirit creates a kind of beauty the most expensive creams and intensive exercise programs can never produce. An unfading inner beauty is pleasing to God and our husbands.

> There is nothing more beautiful than a woman with a gentle and quiet spirit.

Now read 1 Peter 3:5–6.

Peter cites Sarah as an example of a wife submitting to her husband. However, it appears Sarah didn't always know her place. She had a tendency to take matters into her own hands as a young woman. In fact, Sarah's original name was Sarai. The name was the Hebrew word *Saray*, and it meant "dominative." Let's take a look at an example of Sarai living up to her name.

Please read Genesis 16:1–6.

Sarai certainly wasn't displaying any signs of that gentle and quiet spirit for which Peter commended her. She was angry she didn't have any children. She felt sorry for herself and was determined to build a family—her way. Sarai told Abraham to go and sleep with Hagar, and he did.

Women have great influence over their husbands, don't they? I imagine Sarai held quite a pity party as she explained her plan to start a family. Abraham submitted to Sarai. His submission to her caused strife and conflict.

Years later, Sarai's name was changed to Sarah. She had grown and matured. Having dealt with the consequences of her dominative behavior, she made some changes. Peter tells us Sarah then called Abraham "Master."

How does Genesis 18:10–12 support Peter's statement?

_____

_____

I'd like to share some comments I found about a couple of verses from the Torah (the first five books of the Old Testament, a collection of the Jewish law and history):

> Abraham's wife honored him and called him "lord," for it is written that Sarah said, "My lord is old" (Genesis 18:12). But conversely, God commanded Abraham to honor his wife by calling her "princess," for that is the meaning of her Hebrew name 'Sarah' (Genesis 17:15)."[46]

Doesn't that just bless you? We think we will be giving up something if we "submit" to our husbands. Yet, just as Sarah received the blessing of a husband who called her "princess," I believe we too will hear our husbands speak highly of us as we develop gentle and quiet spirits.

Now read 1 Peter 3:7.

Husbands also have a role to fulfill in marriage. They are to be considerate and respectful to their wives. Although we are physically, and sometimes emotionally, weaker than our husbands, these verses do not imply we are less capable or less intelligent. We are simply to show respect for our husbands and be gentle and quiet in spirit, knowing our place. As we grow, our husbands will begin to recognize our unfading beauty. And, might I suggest, your husband may just surprise you one day by calling you "princess"!

> Although we are physically, and sometimes emotionally, weaker than our husbands, these verses do not imply we are less capable or less intelligent.

WEEK NINE

A Shepherd's Heart

Be shepherds of God's flock that is under your care, serving as overseers—
not because you must, but because you are willing.

1 PETER 5:2

Today we are going to focus on a subject dear to Peter's heart: shepherding the flock. As Peter wrote on this subject, I imagine his mind flashed back to the shore of Galilee.

Let's go there ourselves for a moment. Re-read John 21:12–17.

So much had happened since that day at the sea with Jesus. Peter had grown by leaps and bounds, as had the church. Feeding and caring for the flock are the responsibilities of a shepherd. For the church to operate properly, then and now, leaders need to operate as shepherds.

Read 1 Peter 5:1–4.

Peter wrote specifically to elders, but anyone in a leadership position within the church needs to act as a shepherd to the flock, "not because you must, but because you are willing." Let's explore what Scripture has to say about the role of a shepherd.

Please read Ezekiel 34:1–4.

What do you learn from these verses about the responsibility of a shepherd?

_____

_____

_____

A shepherd has a heart for the flock. The greatest example of someone with a shepherd's heart was Jesus Himself. Many of Jesus' parables are recorded for us in Scripture. Among my favorites is the parable of the lost sheep. It gives a vivid image of the heart of our Chief Shepherd.

> A shepherd has a heart for the flock. The greatest example of someone with a shepherd's heart was Jesus Himself.

Please read Luke 15:3–6.

Can you picture Jesus joyfully placing lost members of His flock upon His shoulders and carrying them home? There are times when leaders in the church need to seek out a lost member of the flock. Our concern for the well-being of each member is part of having a shepherd's heart. A shepherd is active, not passive. The shepherd leads, feeds, and strengthens his flock, reins in strays, and searches for the lost.

Now read 1 Peter 5:5–7 from the King James Version:

> Likewise, ye younger, submit yourselves unto the elder. Yea, all *of you* be subject one to another, and be clothed with humility: for God resisteth the proud, and giveth grace to the humble. Humble yourselves therefore under the mighty hand of God, that he may exalt you in due time: Casting all your care upon him; for he careth for you. (emphasis added)

A wise shepherd humbles himself before God and submits totally to His authority. Once again, we can look to Jesus as our example.

Please read Philippians 2:1–8.

If Jesus, "being in very nature God," could humble Himself under the mighty hand of God, even to the point of dying on the cross, shouldn't we strive to humble ourselves in the common situations of our lives?

I had a cervical fusion several years ago due to a neck injury I had sustained as a child in a car accident. The procedure involved removing a disk from my neck and replacing it with a piece of bone. The disk had been compressing my spinal cord and some other nerves. After the surgery, I continued to have problems with numbness and pain. About a year after the surgery, the pain was so severe I thought I was heading for another surgery.

I was determined to find alternative methods of treatment. I have two close friends who have seen a chiropractor regularly for years. They urged me to get some feedback from him. I was terrified. As I drove to the office, I prayed that God would use the man's hands to relieve my pain.

WEEK NINE

I'll never forget that first visit. As the doctor placed his hands on my neck and back, I kept silently praying that prayer. He made several adjustments, some of them painful. God used that visit, and subsequent others, to teach me what it meant to humble myself under God's mighty hand. But over many months, God indeed used those hands to relieve my pain.

To be a good shepherd, we must be completely submissive under God's mighty hand. We can't fight Him; we can't pull against the adjustments He is making in our hearts and lives. Some may be painful, but any changes God makes are necessary and beneficial. As He works on us, we are better able to lead the flock, just as our Chief Shepherd leads us. If we stray from the Shepherd, we have the potential to lead others astray as well.

For our final reading today, please read 1 Peter 5:8–14.

As believers, we need to exercise self-control and be alert to the fact that we have an enemy who desires to destroy our testimonies. We have to stand firm in our faith so our enemy doesn't have much with which to work. When we fail, which we will all do, we can take comfort in knowing that one day our God will fully restore all of us in His eternal kingdom.

> As believers, we need to exercise self-control and be alert to the fact that we have an enemy who desires to destroy our testimonies.

What lessons did you learn from Peter this week that will remain with you when you finish this study?

_____

_____

_____

_____

_____

Personal Application

Application for Day One

To begin today, let's revisit some passages we studied this week on Day One.

Please re-read 1 Peter 1:6–7.

What does verse 6 indicate we will suffer while we are here on Earth?

_____

_____

The Greek word translated "trials" in verse 6 is *peirasmos*. It means "a putting to proof (by experiment of good, experience of evil, solicitation, discipline or provocation); by implication adversity; temptation."

We experience trials of various kinds while we are on this earth. Some are caused by circumstances outside our control. Some, however, are the result of either poor choices or outright rebellion.

Re-read verse 6 and replace the word "trials" with "temptations."

We can count on eventually experiencing grief when we succumb to temptation. Think back to one particular choice you made that has caused you the most regret or resulted in the greatest consequences. Write down one word that represents that sin:

_____

_____

_____

The word *tempt* is defined as "to induce or persuade by enticement or allurement, as to do something unwise, wrong, or immoral."[47] Think back on the situation you listed above. What emotion or weakness (e.g., pride, loneliness, anger) in your life made you susceptible to being enticed or persuaded?

_____

_____

_____

One way to protect ourselves from being enticed to the same sin again and again is to analyze the circumstances that made us susceptible in the first place. Continue to analyze the conditions until you can recognize what made you vulnerable. Then acknowledge your vulnerability next time and ask God to help you guard against temptation.

> One way to protect ourselves from being enticed to the same sin again and again is to analyze the circumstances that made us susceptible in the first place.

Read 1 Corinthians 10:13.

The Greek word translated "temptation" in this verse is the same *peirasmos* we just saw translated "trial(s)" in 1 Peter 1:6. There is no temptation that God will allow to be placed before us that is beyond our ability to resist. God Himself will provide a way out, but it is up to us to search for it.

Take a moment to again analyze the situation you listed. What could you have done differently? What escape did God provide? Ask God to help you clearly see the way out next time. Then look for it!

Application for Day Two

Peter began to separate himself from the Gentile Christians because he feared criticism from the Jewish Christians. Refresh your memory by reading Galatians 2:11–13.

I have great compassion for Peter. He made a mistake I make on a regular basis. He put too much emphasis on the approval of men. Do you do that, too?

What does Galatians 1:10 tell us about seeking the approval of men?

_____

_____

When we say or do things to seek approval from others, we are not being servants of Christ. We are only serving ourselves. When our motive is acceptance from others, we are only trying to advance our position, increase our circle of friends, or make ourselves look good. All those motives are self-focused.

The word translated "servant" in Galatians 1:10 technically means "slave," which is defined as "one who is the property of and wholly subject to another; a bond servant."[48] We cannot be "wholly subject" to God if we are looking out for our own interests by seeking the approval of others.

In addition to the areas you are currently serving in the body of Christ, I would like to challenge you to perform an act of service next week, either for your church or for a member of your church/community. I'd like to suggest you make sure the act of service is something for which you stand to gain absolutely nothing. No recognition. No personal benefit. Perform the service anonymously. Ask God to reveal what you should do and keep your eyes open for an opportunity. Have fun with this assignment. Your only boundary is to make sure the only benefit or recognition you receive is the smile of your heavenly Father.

> In addition to the areas you are currently serving in the body of Christ, I would like to challenge you to perform an act of service next week, either for your church or for a member of your church/community.

You stand to gain recognition if you share your act of service with your small group, so please don't share this exercise with anyone. Keep it between you and God and have fun being a blessing!

Application for Day Three

Our focus passage for Day Three was 1 Peter 3:3–4. I've written it below from the New Living Translation:

> Don't be concerned about the outward beauty of fancy hairstyles, expensive jewelry, or beautiful clothes. You should clothe yourselves instead with the beauty that comes from within, the unfading beauty of a gentle and quiet spirit, which is so precious to God.

I like the word "concerned" in this translation. We often spend far too much time worrying about what we're going to wear or how we look. We feel insecure when we have a "bad hair day." But Peter says those earthly concerns will one day fade away. Our hair turns gray, our clothes wear out, our jewelry eventually tarnishes. But the inner beauty of a gentle and quiet spirit never fades.

Peter wasn't saying we should all walk around without jewelry, makeup, or clean clothing. He didn't ever say women should dress plainly. Our focus should be on developing inner beauty. Our outward dress should simply be an expression of our taste and personality. Our fashion or style shouldn't have anything to do with our self-worth.

Do you find Peter's words convicting? If so, explain:

_____

_____

_____

_____

Application for Day Four

Is there someone you know whom you would consider a lost sheep? Perhaps it is someone who has strayed from the church or is caught in a pattern of sin or rebellion.

> Is there someone you know whom you would consider a lost sheep?

Ask God to help you know how to reach out to that person. You might write a note to someone you haven't seen at church for a while. Or make a phone call and invite a neighbor to church. Be creative. If you're uncomfortable, ask a leader in your small group for some guidance on shepherding.

Re-read Luke 15:3–6 for some guidance from our Chief Shepherd. Summarize His parable in your own words:

_____

_____

_____

_____

_____

_____

I encourage you to reach out to lost sheep. This time, share your experience with the members of your small group. It is encouraging to hear how others shepherd lost or straying sheep. There is no set formula. There will be as many approaches as women in your group, but we all need to care for the flock by going after lost sheep.

WEEK NINE

Week 10

Abandoning Self for Christ

Blessed Invitation

*Everything that goes into a life of pleasing God has been miraculously
given to us by getting to know, personally and intimately,
the One who invited us to God.*

2 PETER 1:3 MSG

It is difficult to believe that this is our final week of study together. For the next few days, we will study the second of Peter's letters included in Scripture. Peter chose to address this letter to anyone who has "received a faith as precious" as his (2 Peter 1:1). I pray you will read this letter as though you had pulled it from your mailbox.

Begin by reading 2 Peter 1:1–4 from your Bible, and then read verses 3 and 4 from *The Message*:

Everything that goes into a life of pleasing God has been miraculously given to us by getting to know, personally and intimately, the One who invited us to God. The best invitation we ever received! We were also given absolutely terrific promises to pass on to you—your tickets to participation in the life of God after you turned your back on a world corrupted by lust.

Everything we need to live out our lives in a manner pleasing to God is gained through a personal and intimate relationship with Jesus Christ. Peter had that kind of relationship with His Lord. He knew Jesus personally. That relationship enabled Peter to be the "Rock" of the early church and to have an impact on the lives of others. Peter's relationship with Jesus also gave him the ability to stand firm and not be shaken by the corruption that surrounded him.

> Everything we need to live out our lives in a manner pleasing to God is gained through a personal and intimate relationship with Jesus Christ.

When we are in a relationship, we feel a connection with the other person. Peter's relationship with Jesus manifested itself in three ways: Peter was connected to Christ emotionally and spiritually; he associated with Jesus continually from the moment he became a disciple; and he was actively involved in Jesus' ministry.

Are you connected to Jesus? Do you feel a bond with Him? Do you associate with Him regularly through prayer and worship? Are you involved with Him in ministering to others? Prayerfully and honestly consider each of these aspects of your relationship and write your thoughts:

_____

_____

_____

_____

God loves you dearly. He desires for you to know Him intimately through Jesus. He knows you intimately.

To encourage you and confirm that point, please read Psalm 139:1–14 out loud and note the three assurances that mean the most to you at this time:

1. _____

2. _____

3. _____

Hebrews 8 talks about the new covenant we have through Christ. Please read verses 8 through 12 and note the evidence you find confirming God's desire for you to know Him intimately:

_____

_____

_____

Peter allowed Jesus to wipe him clean of his sins and he experienced true forgiveness. As Peter walked with Jesus, he didn't walk five steps behind with his head hung low. He didn't watch from a distance, hoping to catch a word or two as Jesus spoke with others. Peter walked tall while with Jesus. He talked with Jesus, he ministered beside Him, and he learned from Him. This relationship strengthened Peter and gave him the courage and perseverance to remain faithful and steady as a leader of the early church. That same type of relationship is available to you and to me. In that we can greatly rejoice!

> Peter allowed Jesus to wipe him clean of his sins and he experienced true forgiveness.

Now read 2 Peter 1:5–9.

In order to escape the corruption of this world, Peter urges us to develop several distinct character traits. According to verses 5 through 7, what are those character traits? (I've listed the first one for you.)

1. Goodness

2. _____

3. _____   _____

4. _____

5. _____

6. _____   _____

7. _____

Peter advises us to develop these aspects of our character in "increasing measure," continually growing and developing so we will be effective and fruitful in our Christian walk. Most of these character traits are part of the fruit of the Spirit, which we discussed earlier in our study. Let's take a closer look at two character traits not part of the fruit of the Spirit: knowledge and godliness.

The Greek word translated "knowledge" in 2 Peter 1:5 is *gnosis*. It comes not from intellectual pursuits, but through the Holy Spirit. It is focused on the Person and Word of God.[49]

The Greek word translated "godliness" in this verse is *eusebeia,* and it is the "proper conduct that springs from a right relationship with God. It is not right action done from a sense of duty, but the spontaneous virtue that comes from the indwelling of Christ and reflects Him."[50]

So when you combine our definitions it is clear that godliness springs from a right relationship built upon the knowledge of Christ through God's Word. The key to being a fruitful Christian is a relationship.

Please read 2 Peter 1:10–11 from your Bible and then read the interpretation as recorded in *The Message:*

> So, friends, confirm God's invitation to you, his choice of you. Don't put it off; do it now. Do this, and you'll have your life on a firm footing, the streets paved and the way wide open into the eternal kingdom of our Master and Savior, Jesus Christ.

You have been invited into a personal and intimate relationship with Jesus. Have you accepted that invitation? That relationship is available, and Peter told us it is developed through knowledge of Jesus gained by spending time in His Word. In other words, like any other relationship, it takes work.

Let's continue reading Peter's letter. Please read 2 Peter 1:12–15.

The one-time Galilean fisherman's greatest passion as a leader of the church was for the flock (including you) to remember the need for relationship. As Peter wrote, he knew his life was soon coming to an end. It was his deepest desire that everyone who received a faith as precious as his would have the same personal and intimate relationship he had experienced.

> The one-time Galilean fisherman's greatest passion as a leader of the church was for the flock (including you) to remember the need for relationship.

Please read 2 Peter 1:16–21.

Peter was an eyewitness to the miraculous power of Jesus and he had experienced the majesty of Jesus firsthand. One day, Jesus will return and all believers will witness the fullness of His glory and majesty. Peter (along with James and John) was privileged to witness a preview of that day on the Mount of Transfiguration.

God gave clues centuries earlier through the words of the prophets about the events of Jesus' first and second comings. Young Jewish boys were taught about prophecy as they studied the Scriptures in school, and they were anxiously watching for the Messiah. I can't imagine how exciting it must have been for Peter to recognize the fulfillment of those prophecies he had studied as a child.

What does 2 Timothy 3:16 tell us about all Scripture?

_____

All Scripture is God-breathed and, as Peter says, "You will do well to pay attention to it, as to a light shining in a dark place" (2 Peter 1:19).

What does Psalm 119:105 call the Word of God?

_____

A lamp lights our way in the darkness, but once the sun comes up, our lamps are dim in comparison. Peter tells us we will do well to focus on the Word to bring light to our hearts. But one day, when Jesus returns, the light we have now will be dim in comparison. At that time, Jesus, the bright Morning Star, will rise up in our hearts and the fullness of Jesus will far outshine all we can possibly know of Him now. The relationship we develop with our Savior here on Earth is only a preview of what we will experience in heaven.

Read Revelation 22:12–17.

Peter was an eyewitness to the majesty (magnificence, splendor, glory, and mighty power) of Jesus Christ. He got a preview of his Master's glory and splendor that will only be fully revealed when Jesus one day returns. Each of us has been invited to have a personal and intimate relationship with Jesus Christ. It is a blessed invitation from a gracious and compassionate Lord.

WEEK TEN

A Lesson from the Mud

*If they have escaped the corruption of the world by knowing our Lord and
Savior Jesus Christ and are again entangled in it and overcome, they are
worse off at the end than they were at the beginning.*

2 PETER 2:20

Peter writes that the words of the prophets had been written through the inspiration
of the Holy Spirit. Peter then gives us a strong warning as relevant today as it was
when Peter penned this letter.

Begin today by reading 2 Peter 2:1–3.

There were false prophets in Israel and false teachers
within the churches. Deception has always been a powerful tool used by Satan to undermine God's relationship
with His people. The Greek word translated "introduce" in
verse 1 is *pareisago*. It means "to lead in aside; i.e., introduce surreptitiously; privily bring in."

> Deception has
> always been a
> powerful tool
> used by Satan to
> undermine God's
> relationship with His
> people.

False teachers don't innocently teach something in error.
They twist the Word of God and teach something "aside
(a short distance apart)" from truth. There is just enough
truth in their teaching to make it sound familiar and some-
what comfortable. But in reality, their teaching tears away
at the fabric of our faith until we are unable to discern truth from lie, right from wrong.
According to Peter, these false teachers do it intentionally in order to gain fame and money.

We discussed this before, but it is imperative we look Scriptures up for ourselves and
double-check what we are taught, particularly if a teacher is continually telling us what we
want to hear.

What does Hebrews 4:12 tell you about God's Word?

_____

_____

When teaching continually sounds great and makes you feel good, proceed with caution. Peter made it clear that God does not allow those who intentionally deceive His people with their teaching to go unpunished. Our next reading gives a few examples of how God deals with that kind of deceitful behavior.

Please read 2 Peter 2:4–19.

I don't know about you, but I think these passages are among the most disturbing in Scripture. I am overcome with emotion as I think of someone I once knew whose actions might line up with some of the behavior outlined in these passages. I'm crying out to God, praising Him for the mercy I've received (I certainly have sinned and fallen short on many occasions), and asking Him to be merciful toward those who are "slaves to depravity."

Their behavior is treacherous and harmful. According to verse 18, whom do these people entice?

_____

_____

Those most vulnerable to false teaching are new believers. Those who are new in the faith do not have the discernment or knowledge to recognize the lies mixed in with the truth. Deceiving someone who is without knowledge of God's Word is one of Satan's common tactics. The way we ward off His schemes is developing a strong knowledge of Scripture. The best way to recognize truth is to study it.

> Those most vulnerable to false teaching are new believers.

Interestingly, the Secret Service investigates counterfeiting of currency in the United States. Guess what they recommend the general public do to guard against being fooled by counterfeit bills: Be familiar with the real thing. The more familiar we are with real money—its marks, its color, its texture—the better we are able to recognize a counterfeit.

Likewise, the more familiar we are with God's Word—the more we study it, memorize it, and recognize it—the more we will be able to identify false or counterfeit teaching.

WEEK TEN

Peter has a little more to say about those new believers who are enticed away by false teachers.

Please read 2 Peter 2:20–22.

Why do you think Peter says those who are again entangled in the corruption of the world after experiencing Jesus are worse off than if they'd never left that corruption?

_____

_____

Once you've experienced being scrubbed clean by Jesus Christ, you're never again satisfied with wallowing in the mud. You know there is something better. You recognize as a child of God you shouldn't be there. The mud may be familiar, but you've been cleaned up and the mud doesn't feel good anymore.

Peter knew what he was talking about. He had denied Jesus. In fact, he had denied Him three times in a very short time span. And Peter had attempted to return to his old life.

Read 2 Peter 2:1:

> But there were also false prophets among the people, just as there will be false teachers among you. They will secretly introduce destructive heresies, even *denying the sovereign Lord who bought them*—bringing swift destruction on themselves. (emphasis added)

Sometimes we shy away from speaking out against mistakes we have made ourselves. We fear being called hypocrites or think our words will have little impact on those who know us and are aware of our mistakes. But Peter knew what denying the One who bought him was all about. Peter had experienced the rebuke of the apostle Paul when he himself was influenced by improper teaching and led others astray by his example. Peter knew the dangers of denying Christ. He had witnessed the effect of improper teaching.

Peter's words in the second chapter of this letter are a passionate warning to members of the church. Anytime we are serving ourselves, we are, in effect, denying Christ. Peter had served himself in the enemy's courtyard. He had denied Jesus to protect his own interests. He had served his own interests as he dined with some misled Jewish Christians, segregating the Gentiles. His actions caused confusion and division within the church. Peter had professed to love Jesus more than anyone. But even in that, the focus had been on himself.

Peter had been forgiven and restored. With his restoration came the passion for protecting the flock from others who would lead them astray.

As members of the flock, we need to be careful who we follow. Sheep are known to follow anyone who leads. We need to choose our leaders carefully. And leaders need to constantly evaluate their motives and make sure they are serving Christ, not themselves.

> As members of the flock, we need to be careful who we follow.

Peter had never intentionally led God's people astray, but he had made some mistakes. God used Peter mightily to warn the church to avoid those same mistakes.

What mistakes have you made that could be used to minister to and warn the flock?

_____

_____

_____

What does James 3:1 tell you about teachers?

_____

_____

God holds teachers to a higher level of accountability than others. There have been times when I've read that verse and I've wanted to walk away from teaching, never to write another lesson. But I can't do that without being disobedient to God. Peter wasn't telling teachers to put down their pens or cancel their classes. He was warning us to be careful what we teach. Our heavenly Father doesn't take rebellion or false teaching lightly. It may appear that some people get away with it for a time, but Scripture teaches us that those who are "slaves to corruption" and intentionally lead the flock astray will be punished. Let's be on our guard, lest we find ourselves heading for some slimy, witness-stealing mud.

> God holds teachers to a higher level of accountability than others.

A Heavenly Stroll

The city does not need the sun or the moon to shine on it, for the glory of God gives it light, and the Lamb is its lamp.

REVELATION 21:23

Yesterday Peter gave us a strong warning about false teachers within the church. He taught us they will be held accountable when Jesus returns. Peter then launched into the topic of Jesus' second coming. Let's see what Peter had to say.

Please read 2 Peter 3:1–9.

According to verse 9, what is the reason Jesus has not yet returned?

_____

_____

_____

This life is often difficult, and for those of us who look forward to our eternal home in heaven, the wait can seem far too long. But our heavenly Father tarries because His deepest desire is for everyone to come to repentance and salvation through Jesus Christ.

On September 11, 2001, I was working on the 47th floor of an office building in downtown Houston. I remember the shock of hearing what was taking place at the World Trade Center in New York. After scrambling for information, my employer closed the office, concerned Houston might be among the next targets. I rode home with my husband, Mark, who also worked downtown at the time. When we got home, we immediately turned on the television, just in time to see the first of the World Trade Center towers implode and tumble to the ground.

All I could think of, as I watched one floor collapse onto another, was people. People such as those I worked with every day. People such as those I saw in the elevators or walking through the hallways. The people had faces and families. They had stopped by a bakery in a food court that morning for a muffin and coffee, just as I had. They had gotten irritated over a slow elevator or taken the stairs for some exercise. The images haunted me for days. I remember being so grief-stricken at one point that I tearfully prayed that the Lord would just come back and end all the suffering.

Then, I sensed God's gentle correction. What happened in those buildings was horrific. There are no words to adequately describe the tragedy. I feel certain God was deeply grieved over the evil that prevailed that day and the lives that were devastated. But the fact is, if Jesus had returned at that moment, many more would be eternally lost than the number who died in those buildings that day.

God drove home His point to me a few days later. I received a letter from a boy we sponsor in India through Compassion International. The cloud of grief that had hovered over me for days suddenly turned to joy as I read that our sponsored child had accepted Jesus as his Lord and Savior. I couldn't even finish reading his letter through the tears that flowed down my face. God waits because there are many, just like that precious little boy in India, who have not yet secured their place with Him for all eternity.

> God waits because there are many, just like that precious little boy in India, who have not yet secured their place with Him for all eternity.

God is the only One who knows the exact time of Jesus' return. He may not come today or tomorrow, but He will return. Jesus waits at the right hand of the Father for the glorious moment when He is able to return for us as His bride. But the bride is not yet ready. There are still believers to be added, like precious pearls to be fastened to a glorious wedding gown.

Now read 2 Peter 3:10–13.

The earth will be destroyed, but believers in Christ can look forward to a new heaven and a new earth. Let's take a peek at what Scripture tells us about our eternal home.

Please read Revelation 21:1–27.

We, the bride of Christ, will walk on streets of gold by the light of the glory of our God. Is your name in the Book of Life? Will you join us for those heavenly strolls? God

> Is your name in the Book of Life?

tarries because He wants you to walk on those beautiful streets of gold, basking in His glory. Have you accepted His blessed invitation?

If not, would you accept that invitation today? Pray this prayer with me now:

> Heavenly Father, I believe that Jesus is your Son, who came to this earth as a man and died on a cross for my sins. I acknowledge to you that I am a sinner and I need forgiveness. Your Word says in Romans 10:9, "That if [I] confess with [my] mouth, 'Jesus is Lord,' and believe in [my] heart that God raised him from the dead, [I] will be saved." I do believe, Lord, and I take Jesus today as my personal Lord and Savior. Thank you, Father, for saving me. In Jesus' name I pray.

If you prayed that prayer for the first time, please talk to your small group leader or pastor. Rejoice because you are part of the church—the beautiful and precious bride of Jesus. Our Bridegroom is coming!

Let's see what Peter says we should do as we wait on Jesus' return.

Please read 2 Peter 3:14–18.

Peter had been transformed by the grace he received through His relationship with Jesus. He urges us to continue growing in the grace and knowledge of Jesus.

Whom do we learn about as we grow in our knowledge of Jesus, according to John 14:9–10?

Jesus was God in the flesh. When we study the words of Jesus, we hear the very words of God. Jesus' life and His many powerful miracles were only a preview of what we will experience in heaven. Jesus' mercy is a reflection of God's mercy. His compassion is a reflection of God's compassion. His wrath is a reflection of God's wrath. We know the Father by knowing the Son.

Will you accept Peter's challenge? Will you continue to grow in your relationship with Jesus so you can experience deeper levels of His abundant grace and favor? I challenge you to commit now to growing in your knowledge and relationship with Christ after you complete the final page of this Bible study. If you accept that challenge, write a prayer of commitment:

> Will you accept Peter's challenge? Will you continue to grow in your relationship with Jesus so you can experience deeper levels of His abundant grace and favor?

_____

_____

_____

_____

Jesus revealed the righteousness and majesty of God through His life here on Earth. I pray you will grow closer to Him every single day of your life. One day, He will return and we will live forever together with our Lord and Savior in paradise. I look forward to taking heavenly strolls with you surrounded by His glory!

As a way of closing, read Revelation 22:1–5 and rejoice because one day you will see the fullness of His majesty revealed before your very eyes.

WEEK TEN | DAY FOUR

Reckless Abandon

> _"Come, follow me," Jesus said, "and I will make you fishers of men."_
> _At once they left their nets and followed him._
>
> MARK 1:17–18

Peter had abandoned all for Christ, or so it appeared. During today's lesson, we'll reflect on some of Simon Peter's failures and his victories. By exploring our friend Peter's life, we can come to a deeper understanding of what it means to truly abandon self for Christ.

When we first met Peter, he was an ordinary, unschooled fisherman without much distinction. He was a man people probably liked and often waved to as he walked through the town of Capernaum in Galilee on his way to the sea each day—a good ol' boy, as we might call him today. However, when Peter was introduced to the Savior, his entire life changed.

What does Peter say to Jesus in Mark 10:28?

Peter believed he had left everything to follow Jesus. After all, he hadn't put someone in charge of his business while he was gone. Peter simply walked away from the life he'd known in Galilee to follow a Jewish rabbi named Jesus.

And he wasn't the only one. Look back at Mark 1:19–20.

Here James and John were in their boat mending and preparing nets with their father. Jesus walked by and called to them, and they got up and left their father "in the boat with the hired men." They abandoned everything for Jesus. Don't you wonder what their father might have been thinking as his boys walked away?

Let's take a moment to reflect on another key moment in Peter's life.

Read Matthew 14:22–33.

According to verse 29, how did Peter respond when Jesus called him from the water?

Peter left the security of the boat. He risked making himself look foolish in front of his peers. Peter threw caution and reason to the wind and got out of that boat. He continually took risks in his walk with Jesus. Peter appeared to hold nothing back. The other disciples probably ribbed Peter about sinking, but inside they undoubtedly felt just a twinge of envy, wishing they too had experienced that moment of walking on the water with their Lord.

At one point, some who had been following Jesus began to fall away because they thought Jesus' teaching was too difficult to follow. Let's see Peter's reaction.

Please read John 6:60–69.

I would guess some scoffers who might have waved a friendly hello to Peter during his fishing days now made fun of him as he walked around the towns in Galilee. Peter had left his fishing boat, his nets, even his home. As an apostle, Peter was commissioned to spread the gospel and he did that wherever he went. Everyone knew Peter was a follower of Jesus. He was fully convinced Jesus was the "Holy One of God." Jesus was the only One who offered eternal life—Peter left no other options open. He said, in essence, "I have nowhere else to go."

> As an apostle, Peter was commissioned to spread the gospel and he did that wherever he went.

Peter thought he had abandoned all for Christ. Yet when he denied knowing Jesus in the high priest's courtyard, he was confronted with the humbling truth that he had not abandoned everything. Peter had abandoned his earthly possessions. He had left behind a fishing business, his family, even his identity. But Peter had not completely surrendered himself.

Let's take one final trip back to Peter's walk with Jesus. Please read John 21:4–19.

This was a pivotal moment in Peter's life. He had walked away from his life at the sea. But when Jesus said, "Follow me" this time, it was different. This time, it was made very clear Peter would eventually give up his very life if he chose to follow Jesus.

As Peter stood on the shore of the sea with Jesus, what do you suppose he was thinking when he glanced at his fishing boat and nets (representing his life prior to knowing Christ)?

_____

_____

_____

Now imagine the remains of the fire where Peter had been rebuked, then restored over breakfast. What do you think that fire represented to Peter?

_____

_____

_____

Peter had left the boat behind before. I don't believe he had a problem leaving it again. He was far more interested in fishing for men than any fish in that sea. But I believe the fire

WEEK TEN

represented the part of Peter he had withheld from Jesus the first time he'd responded to the words "Follow me." The fire represented the trial that brought Peter's self-interest and selfish ambition to the surface.

Peter had been willing to abandon all for Jesus because he thought Jesus was going to reign as King on Earth. That's what all the disciples believed at first. Peter wasn't willing to die the first time because it seemed to make all he had done and worked for meaningless. He had been working with the anticipation of a reward. Peter loved Jesus deeply, but he had one major obstacle left to get out of the way before he could truly become the man he was created to become. That obstacle was self.

One of Webster's definitions of *self* is "personal interest or advantage."[51]

Peter had not abandoned his "personal interest" the first time he answered the call to follow Jesus. But this time, Peter had a deeper understanding of what it meant to be a disciple. He understood that his rewards would not be earthly ones. He knew that in order to be a disciple, he would have to be willing to lay down his very life. He thought he had done that before, but as he stood on the shore of Galilee this time, he left behind far more than a fishing boat and a net. Peter abandoned self for Christ.

What about you? Have you abandoned self for Christ? Write down your thoughts:

_____

_____

_____

_____

I thank God for Peter's example. The next time the "fires" in our lives reveal selfish ambition or improper motives, we know what we need to do. We simply need to have a humbling breakfast with our Lord. We need to allow Him to confront us with our selfishness and purify us from improper motives. Then we need to again answer the call to follow Jesus, with a greater commitment and understanding of what it means to be His disciple.

> I thank God for Peter's example.

A Fruitful Disciple

"This is to my Father's glory, that you bear much fruit,
showing yourselves to be my disciples."

JOHN 15:8

*I*t's difficult to believe that this is our last lesson together. Yesterday, we discovered we have to abandon self in order to truly follow Jesus. Today's lesson will highlight what it takes to bear the fruit of discipleship.

In Day Three's lesson this week, we got some vivid images of our eternal home. The kingdom of heaven is available to everyone who accepts Jesus as Lord and Savior. As believers in Christ, we can continually look forward to heaven. But with any privilege comes responsibility.

Before we explore our responsibilities as Jesus' disciples, let's look for a moment at a special privilege Jesus gave Peter.

Matthew 16:19 tells us, "I will give you the keys of the kingdom of heaven; whatever you bind on earth will be bound in heaven, and whatever you loose on earth will be loosed in heaven."

Peter was told he would be given the keys to the kingdom of heaven. He was given the responsibility of opening the door leading into the kingdom.

Peter was the first to preach the gospel to the people in Jerusalem at Pentecost, and he was the first to preach to the Gentiles. Jesus appointed Peter to unlock the door to the kingdom of heaven by the power of the Holy Spirit,

> Peter was the first to preach the gospel to the people in Jerusalem at Pentecost, and he was the first to preach to the Gentiles.

and it remains open to all who hear and accept the gospel. But it is not just Peter who was commissioned to spread the gospel.

Please read Matthew 28:16–20.

Whom was Jesus addressing and what did He tell them to do?

_____

_____

If we are followers of Jesus and thus His disciples, we too are commissioned to go and make disciples.

How is this confirmed by John 15:8?

_____

We show ourselves to be Jesus' disciples when we bear fruit and make more disciples. We have the privilege of eternity in heaven and the responsibility of sharing the Good News with others. Peter opened the door. We are commissioned to continually help people find their way through it.

Let's back up for a moment and read John 15:5.

Apart from Jesus Christ, we can do nothing. Jesus tells us He is the "true Vine" and we must remain attached (the King James Version says "abide") in an intimate and personal relationship with Him if we are to bear fruit.

Jesus tells us God is the Gardner. In a garden, if a branch is detached from its life-giving vine, its fruit-bearing season is cut short as it withers and dies. If we are to bear fruit, living a life that identifies us as Jesus' disciples, we have to be in constant relationship with Him. Just as a branch depends on its vine for nourishment and water, so must we depend upon Jesus Christ.

Jesus is the Word of God and the Bread of Life. If we are to bear fruit, we need to nourish ourselves with God's Word—our daily Bread.

How is the Lord described in the final line of Jeremiah 17:13?

_____

Jesus is not only our daily Bread, He is our living Water. As we remain in a relationship with Him, He quenches our thirst and we thrive as a rich and healthy branch. Jesus died so we could have a relationship with Him. A rich and rewarding relationship with the Savior doesn't come from just attending church every Sunday or praying over your food every day. It takes effort and time. Learning about our Lord through Bible study, walking with Him (being obedient to His Word), and talking with Him in prayer on a consistent basis will help you become a rich and fruitful disciple.

Peter loved Jesus with such intensity he was overzealous at times. His passion was a result of continually growing in his knowledge of Jesus. Peter walked with Jesus and talked with Him on a daily basis. Peter was always asking questions and He desired to know all he could about his Lord.

As he closed his second letter, Peter urged us to grow in the grace and knowledge of Jesus. That is exactly what we have watched Peter do as we traveled with him through this study. May the apostle Peter be a source of encouragement to you as you remember his victories as well as his failures. May you find comfort as you recognize, through Peter's example, we don't have to be perfect to experience a rich relationship with Jesus Christ.

> Peter loved Jesus with such intensity he was overzealous at times. His passion was a result of continually growing in his knowledge of Jesus.

To end our lesson today, I'd like to share an excerpt from *The New Foxe's Book of Martyrs*. This is believed to be an accurate account of Peter's death:

> "When Peter was old, Nero planned to put him to death. When the disciples heard of this, they begged Peter to flee the city [said to be Rome], which he did. But when he got to the city gate, he saw Christ walking toward him. Peter fell to his knees and said, 'Lord, where are you going?' Christ answered, 'I've come to be crucified again.' By this, Peter understood that it was his time to suffer the death of Jesus which would glorify God (John 21:19). So he went back to the city. After being captured and taken to his place of martyrdom, he requested that he be crucified in an upside down position because he did not consider himself worthy to be crucified in the same position as his Lord."[52]

Assuming this account is correct, Peter did it right in the end. He didn't fail; he didn't deny his Lord. He bravely died as a martyr to glorify God. With the same humility we have come to adore in Peter, he asked to be crucified upside down, not feeling worthy to be in the same position as His Lord and beloved Friend.

When we first met Peter, he was eager and impulsive. He was quick to speak and often acted without thinking. But through his relationship with Jesus and the power of the Holy

WEEK TEN

Spirit, we saw Peter transformed. His weaknesses became strengths, and although he still struggled at times, Peter became a man who was stable and strong, courageously devoted to Christ. Peter was a fruitful disciple. His life was a testimony of the fact that he had a relationship with Jesus and was a true disciple. Dear friend, that same relationship is available to you. Seek Him with all your heart!

I pray through our study you have grown in grace (divine influence on your heart) and knowledge of Jesus Christ. I am specifically praying you will bear much fruit, declaring to the world you are His disciple.

It was a privilege to take this journey with you. I am a fellow sojourner in this life and look forward to walking with our Lord and you in our eternal home. Until then, I pray you will put aside any selfish ambition or desire and abandon yourself totally to Christ. May you eat daily of the Bread of Life of God's Word. May you drink freely from the Spring of Living Water that dwells within your heart as a believer. Jesus is life! Abide in Him and you will bear much fruit!

May you, like Peter, be transformed by your glimpse of the majesty of Christ.

We did not follow cleverly invented stories when we told you about the power and coming of our Lord Jesus Christ, but we were eyewitnesses of his majesty.

2 PETER 1:16

END NOTES

1. *The Student Bible* (Grand Rapids, MI: Zondervan, 1986).

2. John F. Walvoord and Roy B. Zuck, *The Bible Knowledge Commentary, New Testament,*(Colorado Springs: Chariot Victor Publishing, 1983), 95.

3. Merrill C. Tenny and J. D. Douglas, *New International Bible Dictionary* (Grand Rapids, MI: Zondervan, 1987), 303.

4. Walvoord and Zuck, 114.

5. Lawrence O. Richards, *New International Encyclopedia of Bible Words* (Grand Rapids, MI: Zondervan, 1991), 525.

6. *The Bible Knowledge Key Word Study: The Gospels* (Colorado Springs: Cook Communications Ministries, 2002), 125.

7. *The New International Webster's Concise Dictionary of the English Language,* (Ridgeland, MS: Trident Press International, 1997), 328.

8. Ibid., 525.

9. Tenny and Douglas, 273.

10. Merrill F. Unger, *Concise Bible Dictionary* (Carol Stream, IL: Tyndale House Publishers, 1974), 20.

11. Ralph Gower, *The New Manners and Customs of Bible Times Student Edition* (Chicago: Moody Bible Institute, 2000), 102.

12. *The New International Webster's Concise Dictionary*, 48.

13. Tenny and Douglas, 266–67.

14. Ibid., 849.

15. Elmer Towns, *The Names of Jesus* (Colorado Springs: Accent Publications, 1987), 114.

16. Merrill F. Unger and William White Jr., *Vine's Complete Expository Dictionary of Old and New Testament Words* (Nashville: Thomas Nelson, 1996), 51.

17. *The New International Webster's Concise Dictionary*, 261.

18. Alfred J. Kolatch, *The Jewish Book of Why* (Middle Village, NY: Johnathan David Publishers, 1995), 187.

19. William Barclay, *The Daily Study Bible Series, The Gospel of Matthew Volume 2, Revised Edition* (Louisville, KY: Westminster John Knox Press, 1975), 143.

20. Ibid., 145.

21. *Life Application Study Bible,* (Carol Stream, IL, and Grand Rapids, MI: Tyndale House Publishers and Zondervan Publishing, 1991),Notes, Exodus 22:26, 141.

22. Walvoord and Zuck, 156.

23. Kevin Howard and Marvin Rosenthal, *The Feasts of the Lord* (Nashville: Thomas Nelson, 1997), 139.

24. Walvoord and Zuck,157.

25. Ibid., 161.

26. William Barclay, *At the Last Trumpet,* (Louisville, KY: Westminster John Knox Press, 1998), 32.

27. Ibid., 40.

28. Walvoord and Zuck, 169.

29. Walvoord and Zuck, 175.

30. Howard Marshall, *Last Supper and Lord's Supper* (Vancouver: Regent College Publishing, 2006), 21.

31. Howard and Rosenthal, 58.

32. Ibid., 59.

33. Walvoord and Zuck, 179.

34. Gower, 80.

35. Christopher Morris, *Academic Press Dictionary of Science and Technology,* (San Diego: Academic Press, 1992), 1008.

36. Walvoord and Zuck, 186.

37. Tenny and Douglas, 817.

38. David H. Stern, *Jewish New Testament Commentary* (Clarksville, MD: Jewish New Testament Publications, 1996), 84.

39. Howard and Rosenthal, 90.

40. Ibid., 76.

41. Ibid., 75.

42. Ibid., 90.

43. Alfred Marshall, *The Interlinear NASB–NIV Parallel New Testament in Greek and English,* (Grand Rapids, MI: Zondervan Publishing House, 1993), 354.

44. John Foxe, *The New Foxe's Book of Martyrs* (Gainesville, FL: Bridge-Logos Publishers, 2001), 358–59.

45. Walvoord and Zuck, 853.

46. Stern, 750.

47. *Webster's Encyclopedia Unabridged Dictionary of the English Language* (Beaverton, OR: Dilithium Press, 1989), 1462.

48. Ibid., 1339.

49. Walvoord and Zuck, 865.

50. Tenny and Douglas, 395.

51. *The New International Webster's Concise Dictionary*, 663.

52. Foxe, 7.